SEA POWER IN THE FALKLANDS

The conclusions and opinions contained herein are those of the author alone, and do not necessarily reflect those of anyone else in the whole world.

SEA POWER IN THE FALKLANDS

Charles W. Koburger, Jr.

PRAEGER

PRAEGER SPECIAL STUDIES • PRAEGER SCIENTIFIC

New York • Philadelphia • Eastbourne, UK
Toronto • Hong Kong • Tokyo • Sydney

Library of Congress Cataloging in Publication Data

Koburger, Charles W.
   Sea power in the Falklands.

   Bibliography: p.
   Includes index.
   1. Great Britain. Royal Navy—History—20th century.
2. Falkland Islands War, 1982—Naval operations, British.
3. Falkland Islands War, 1982—Aerial operations, British.
I. Title.
VA454.K6 1984   359.4'8   83-17823
ISBN 0-03-069534-1 (alk. paper)

On the cover:
Left: A U.S. Navy A-4E Skyhawk (Courtesy McDonnell Douglas).
Right, top: A Naval Air Arm Sea Harrier in flight (Ministry of
Defence, London).
Right, bottom: HMS *Hermes* in the South Atlantic (Ministry of
Defence, London).

Published in 1983 by Praeger Publishers
CBS Educational and Professional Publishing
a Division of CBS Inc.
521 Fifth Avenue, New York, NY 10175 USA

© 1983 Praeger Publishers

3456789 052 987654321

Printed in the United States of America
on acid-free paper

To my son . . .

Contents

LIST OF PHOTOGRAPHS

Note: Photographs appear on pages 76-90, following Chapter 6.

LIST OF ABBREVIATIONS

AA	Anti-aircraft
AAW	Anti-air warfare
ARA	Official prefix indicating a commissioned vessel of the Argentine navy
ASW	Anti-submarine warfare
AWACS	Airborne warning and control system
CAP	Combat air patrol
CIWS	Close-in weapon system
CTF	Commander, Task Force
DFC	Distinguished Flying Cross
DSC	Distinguished Service Cross
DSO	Companion of the Distinguished Service Order
ECM	Electronic countermeasure(s)
EEC	European Economic Community
ESM	Electronic support measure(s)
GBE	Knight Grand Cross of the Order of the British Empire
GRT	Gross registered tons
HM	Her Majesty('s)
HMS	Official prefix indicating a commissioned vessel (or station) of the Royal Navy
LADE	Argentine national (military) airline
LCU	Landing craft utility
LSLI	Landing ship luxury Liner
MARAD	U.S. Maritime Administration
MoD	Ministry of Defence

LIST OF ABBREVIATIONS (Continued)

MSC	Military Sealift Command
MV	Prefix designating a commercial motor vessel
NATO	North Atlantic Treaty Organization
OBE	Officer of the Order of the British Empire
PKT	Picket
POW	Prisoner of war
PVC	Polyvinyl chloride
RAF	Royal Air Force
RAS	Replenishment at sea
RFA	Prefix indicating a commissioned vessel of Britain's Royal Fleet Auxiliary
RM	Royal Marines
RMS	Royal mail steamer
RN	Royal Navy
SAS	Special Air Service
SBS	Special Boat Service
SOA	Speed of advance
SS	Prefix designating a commercial steamship
STUFT	Ship(s) taken up from trade
TEZ	Total exclusion zone
TF	Task force
TRALA	Tug, repair, and logistic area
VERTREP	Vertical replenishment
VSTOL	Vertical/short take off/landing

SEA POWER IN THE FALKLANDS

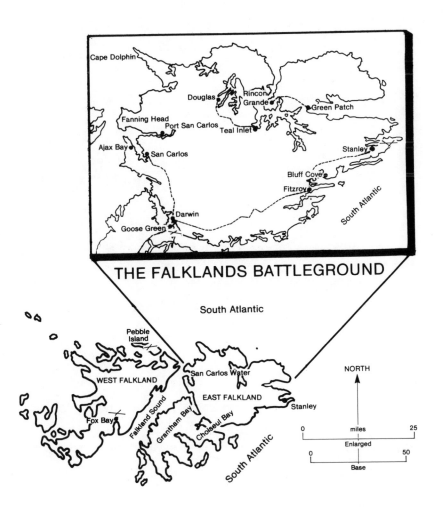

THE FALKLANDS BATTLEGROUND

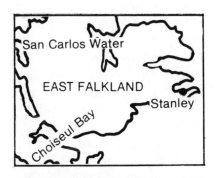

1
Introduction

The 1982 Anglo-Argentine war in the Falklands/Malvinas—regrettable as it has been—offers us a number of valuable clues as to the nature of sea power and especially naval warfare in our time. In our world force is not yet controlled by law, as most know. It would be foolish of us not to examine the Falklands operation from the dispassionate view of the craft of war, and take from it what we can. This preliminary evaluation will attempt to outline these events and begin just such an analysis.

The Anglo-Argentine fight for the Falklands has been brewing for years. It began as a curious nineteenth century–like exercise in the political use of sea power—in gunboat diplomacy—and escalated into the largest sea-air conflict since the Second World War. It became a white-hot naval computer, VSTOL, and missile war, a testing ground for today's newest weapons, organization, strategy, and tactics. It offers us much to study.

This book deals with the preliminary politico-military maneuvering and with the subsequent naval and air battles that swirled around the Falklands, but not with events on land except in the broadest outline. The blockades and landings, however, are covered in detail. They all make a great adventure story, worth reading for that if nothing else.

1

The terms "sea power" and "command of the sea" will appear frequently here. One is the reflection of the other. The ultimate aim of sea power—an overwhelming ideal seldom if ever completely achieved—is command of the sea. Command of the sea is the ability to use the sea, the air above it, and the water beneath it, for one's own purposes, and to deny this use to one's enemy. Command may be just temporary and/or local. Command must be gained, maintained, and exploited; these different aspects tend to require somewhat different tools. It should be noted that command has two sides: a positive (one's own) and a negative (the foe's). Without control of both there is no true command of the sea. Conversely, the proper application of tools—whatever tools, whether the tools are above, on, or below the surface—to accomplish command is sea power.

Ideally sea power is a flexible, general purpose capability. It caters to the widest range of contingencies, and it is not limited strictly to execution of a fixed list of predetermined tasks. Such a list is always one task short, the one immediately faced. Only a good regional (or larger) navy can afford such a traditionally balanced fleet. Smaller navies—stretched too thin—do not have this option.

This book, therefore, deals with sea power—those tools with which to gain, maintain, and exploit command of the sea—not with navies or air forces per se. As will be seen, it is a distortion here to consider just either opposing navy alone. Air forces keep intruding. But sea power is based on a navy—on ships, aircraft, personnel, bases, knowledge, and, above all, a state of mind. One of the most important things the study brings out is the cost of artificially separating surface and air elements in the maritime area. Coordination of these tools if nothing else has to be by the navy. But more on this as we go.

This book is based on near-real-time history, with all of the normal disabilities that go along with that. Official British records of the Falklands affair will not be fully opened for study until the standard 30 years have passed. "White papers" and official reports do help but they are of necessity incomplete. Some information may never be made public.

Without actually providing false information, British officials have apparently withheld facts and perhaps even encouraged

---

Sea power: The ability to influence events at sea, and from the sea.

Command of the sea: The ability to use the sea for one's own purposes, and to deny this ability to one's enemy.

misleading assumptions by the media, presumably to confuse and mislead the Argentines. Some of this misinformation has no doubt been repeated here despite strenuous efforts to correct it. Only time will clear this all up, and time is what we have least of. We shall therefore do the best we can with what we have.

This is not intended to be—nor could it be—an exhaustive "instant history" of the campaign. Only the larger outlines are sketched; enough, it is hoped, with which to set the stage and on which to base our analysis.

Numbers are everywhere avoided. When given, they are to be viewed with a skeptical eye. The British often do not agree even among themselves, and the Argentines provide an occasional disagreement with everyone's figures. When given, numbers are usually only approximate, intended to indicate relative positions, strengths, or losses. They are accurate enough for that, in any case.

Yes, we must indeed be aware all through that we could be drawing inferences from this campaign that are too universal or too categoric. The situation was in many ways too unique for absolutes. The dynamics of technical change are also in many cases too great. But in many other cases the campaign did unquestionably establish new conceptual ground, or confirm trends the first indications of which were already visible, carrying them farther along. Some of the major "lessons" are already there plain for all to see, but many will demand further confirmation.

We were not the only ones watching. The whole world was. Whatever the suffering and dread of ordinary people, military and naval analysts and weapons makers all over must have followed this operation with fascinated concentration. The Soviet naval command must have been particularly interested, for reasons which will become apparent as we go.

The Falklands campaign was primarily a naval one, as we know, conducted over long sea distances. It would appear to help U.S. understanding of these operations in further discussions if we superimposed what happened on our own similar naval experiences in the Pacific during World War II. The British apparently used Ascension Island (a small permanent British air and naval base located just south of the center of the South Atlantic narrows, 3,800 miles away, and shared with the United States) as a very limited equivalent of wartime Hawaii, as a logistics oriented mini-operating base. South Georgia, once it was retaken, became an advanced base, an Espiritu Santo or Saipan. The Falklands themselves were Guadalcanal or the Philippines, as we took them. The parallels are striking, even if the scale was different.

Administratively, as to content, Chapters 2 through 5, most of 7 and the first half of 9 are essentially historical narrative, enough to refresh the memory of an interested reader. Chapter 6 and the rest of 7 and 9 are devoted to operational (''armchair'') analysis, drawing on the narrative. Chapters 8, 10 and 11 attempt to apply some of the insights we have gained to sea power problems of the future. The introduction and conclusion speak for themselves. There are ten appendices, covering more technical matters in detail.

Suggestions are made, aimed primarily at the Royal Navy—the only navy whose air, surface and submarine elements played a significant integrated seapower role—and secondarily at the U.S. Navy. These suggestions are not made with any ideas of instructing either a leading world class navy or its First Sea Lord as to their duties. Royal Navy professionals must know already. These suggestions are addressed rather to an informed and interested public, and perhaps to their political leaders. They cover only the more obvious points, those which were serious enough to appear originally across the sea in the U.S. news media, in terms that it is expected are understandable to all.

Many fine analysts will find their ideas reflected here. The corpus of knowledge on sea power has been worked on for many years. These analysts all have my deepest admiration and most sincere thanks. Two stand out as singularly applicable: Julian Corbett and Edward Luttwak. My debt to them should become clear in the pages that follow. If I see a long way, it is because I too stand on the shoulders of many tall men.

An earlier version of this study appeared as an article in the January 1983 issue of *Navy International*: so did the chapter on Argentina's navy, in May. *Seaways* also published articles based on some of the material. Their permission to use that and other extremely useful material—and for the continuing advice and encouragement received from the U.S. Naval Institute as well as *Navy International* and the (British) Nautical Institute—is gratefully acknowledged.

Acknowledged gratefully also is the unique and considerable factual assistance provided by personnel of the naval attache's office of the Argentine Embassy in Washington. Again, the analysis is all mine. So are any errors.

Most of the photographic illustrations were obtained through the courtesy of the U.S. Naval Institute and the Royal Navy.

In the end, it must be recognized that in the Falklands campaign the British, in their first experience of battle in the missile age, carried off what could rationally have been an impossible operation. They did it with great courage and expertise, in the best tradition of the Royal Navy. Some indications of the nature of war in our time from all this are becoming visible. In another naval war between two such civilized opponents, any time in the near future, this operation will provide a most useful professional model. It adds to the record as well as showing what good men can do, anytime, anywhere, any place.

There is now time and opportunity to find out what really happened, to fill in some of the details, and to learn whatever useful could be learned from this unfortunate piece of history. In the world as it is, and looks to remain, there is certain to be another such incident, whether we seek it or not. If sea power is involved, we had better be good at it.

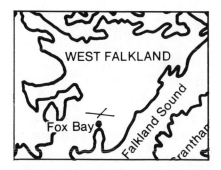

WEST FALKLAND

Fox Bay

Falkland Sound

rantha

2

Historical Background

The Falklands have been a Crown Colony since 1833. They consist of some 200 islands of various sizes, spread over a 150 by 75 nautical mile area between 51° and 53° South and 57°30′ and 62°30′ West. East and West Falklands are the two largest, dominating the group. In total the islands take in some 4,700 hilly, boggy, windy, cold, and largely barren square miles. Together with the sea around them, they provide a quiet sheep-, peat-, seaweed-, and fish-based livelihood for approximately 1,800 people ("kelpers"), almost all of British stock. Port Stanley (on East Falkland) is the capital and, with 1,050 people, the largest town.

These were peaceful islands, somewhat isolated from the outside world and, it seemed, rather preferring to stay that way. The world, however, would not go away and was about to come crashing in.

Economically, the Falklands are company islands, a holdover from an earlier colonial era. More than 40 percent of the two large islands belong to the London-based Falkland Islands Company. The sole bank is owned by the same London firm. The only cargo ship that regularly serviced the islands—coming across every three months—was chartered by it. Steps had been begun to open up the economy, and to integrate it with that of the nearby mainland, but the kelpers had no desire to change their flag. Rather, the contrary seems clearly true.

Argentina—the natural metropole—nonetheless exerted a mounting economic and social attraction, and now was connected by a regular air service.

Glacial South Georgia (800 miles to the southeast) was never part of the Falklands, but with the decline in whaling was, and is an only, seasonly inhabited dependency administered from Stanley for convenience. So are the totally uninhabited South Sandwich Islands, farther to the southeast.

The violent storms which regularly lash the far South Atlantic, screaming angrily out of the Antarctic seas, are known to mariners everywhere. Beginning at the Roaring Forties, these storms strike with little or no warning, their howling winds churning the water into tremendous foaming waves and stinging spray, increasing the islands' normal isolation. The farther south, the worse these storms get.

Possession of these islands had been contested by France, Spain, and England in the early years, and they were finally left uninhabited. Argentina became an independent republic in 1816, assuming title to those territories formerly ruled or claimed by Spain from Buenos Aires. The Falklands/Malvinas was one of these, but remained unoccupied until 1820, when the new government commissioned David Jewitt, an American soldier of fortune fighting for Argentina, to plant the new flag. Jewitt arrived in the islands commanding the Argentine frigate *Heroina,* and duly took possession in the name of Argentina.

Then appeared on the scene one Luis (or Louis) Vernet, a merchant adventurer from Hamburg. In 1822 he obtained from Argentina a monopoly over Falklands fishing and sealing, establishing a settlement in 1826. Buenos Aires used the islands as Spain had done before—as a penal colony. In 1829 Vernet was appointed governor in a move that sounds exactly as if he needed some protection for his claims, and was given the authority to provide it himself if he could.

Interestingly enough, the United States once played a direct part in all this. In 1831 the Argentine governor of the Falklands (still Luis Vernet) seized three U.S. fishing schooners for non-compliance with Argentine fishing regulations and nonpayment of duties. When *Harriet* was brought in to Buenos Aires for trial, the U.S. consul sailed our corvette *Lexington* to the islands to recover her confiscated property. Commodore Silas Duncan put a naval landing party ashore at Port Louis (near the present Stanley) on East Falkland and, in what can perhaps be described as an excess of zeal, the men looted houses, arrested some of the inhabitants as pirates, and took seven of them away in chains. Declaring the islands without government, Duncan then left. Diplomatic relations between the two republics were suspended.

With the collapse of the Vernet regime, the islands were again considered available for claim. When two years later the British claimed their right and took them over, Captain James Onslow with *Clio* and *Tyne* forcing a small garrison to surrender and reestablishing a prior claim, the issue between the United States and Argentina died a natural if slow death.

Held by the British for a century and a half, the Falkland Islands have considerable strategic, commercial and emotional importance. It was here that Vice Admiral Doveton Sturdee's battle cruisers destroyed von Spee's squadron in 1914, and Commodore Henry Harwood assembled his squadron before the defeat of *Graf Spee* in 1939. Once the nineteenth century coaling station was closed, however, the islands were no longer formally used as a naval base.

Not until 1945 did Argentina formally reopen the question of sovereignty, motivated undoubtedly by a combination of factors. The Falklands are claimed by them on the basis of their tangled earlier history, and the Falklands are the key to the other islands. Also a factor is the position of the islands in relation to future claims to large portions of inhospitable but mineral-rich Antarctica, and to South Polar marine resources such as krill. Oil may be another important resource, not only in Antarctica but more immediately on the shelf extending from the islands to the Patagonian (southern) mainland. Strategically, the Falklands completely dominate the Argentine coast, lying for much of the distance loosely in the center of a 400 mile radius arc.

Territorial claims in Antarctica are generally based on ownership of contiguous land, giving each claimant a pie-shaped segment (wedge) ending with its tip at the South Pole. Those of Britain and Argentina (and Chile) conflict, as could be guessed, London and Buenos Aires both staking a good part of their claim south from the Falklands. A 1961 14 power Antarctic treaty temporarily internationalizes the area. It provides for a demilitarized nuclear-free Antarctica south of 60° South latitude, and effectively halts further action until 1991, at least.

In Argentina, the Antarctic and South Polar Seas have long been the special province of its navy. The navy has worked for years to reinforce Argentina's claims through an extensive program of exploration, survey, occupation, and scientific research. The navy manned *Almirante Irizar*, a relatively new 13,900 ton Finnish-built icebreaker as well as a number of ice-strengthened support ships, hard evidence of the major commitment to the south. In one long term view, the Argentine navy is the custodian here of their country's future.

Nonetheless, although the British were 8,000 miles away and had been more or less actively trying to arrange some accommodation with Argentina for over 20 years (resistance by the kelpers was one large obstacle), they were naturally concerned with the defense of islands that were still their own. Both Antarctic claims and oil could well have been in the back of their minds. But the Falklands also dominate the far South Atlantic and the eastern approaches to Cape Horn and the Strait of Magellan, a matter of considerably increased importance now that the Panama Canal is to be released by the United States to Panama. (Modern supertankers already cannot fit through the canal and must go around the Horn.) Finally, acquiescing in any seizure of territory by force would set an unfortunate precedent with serious repercussions in such places as Hong Kong, Gibraltar, and Belize.

By early 1975 relations between the two countries had deteriorated to the point that both ambassadors were recalled over the issue. In 1976 an Argentine destroyer fired a shot across the bows of a British ship in disputed water, and in 1977 the British labor government secretly sent a small naval task group (two frigates and a submarine) to the Falklands to forestall any Argentine attempt at a *coup de main,* holding the group at sea about 400 miles off.

London at this point even drew up rules of engagement and the boundaries of an exclusion zone 25 miles around the islands. The situation then eased. Further escalation was avoided, the ships were withdrawn, and relations restored, more or less.

However, Anglo-Argentine relations soon became dangerously strained. The 150th anniversary of British occupation was fast approaching. The problem came to a head over unauthorized operations by Argentine salvors in South Georgia waters, where at Leith the salvors ran up the Argentine flag and where the real question soon resolved itself into that of whose writ ran there. When the salvors on South Georgia were finally officially asked to leave aboard ARA *Bahia Buen Suceso,* a chartered Argentine naval transport already in the area, they refused.

Her Majesty's Government then sailed RFA *Endurance,* an Antarctic support ship with twenty marines on board to Grytviken, to investigate and if necessary eject the salvors. The Argentines responded with *Bahia Paraiso,* a polar transport carrying 200 of their marines, accompanied by a corvette (*Guerrico*). *Endurance* prudently withdrew, but also remained in the immediate area, keeping the island under observation, to survive for other tasks.

The immediate strategic and economic position of the two nations and their possible dreams of future greatness at this point hung delicately in the balance. So far, despite the admitted movement of several minor diplomatic and naval pawns, nothing absolutely irrevocable had been done. It was not yet too late to work out an accommodation between reasonable people. But things were not to be left at that.

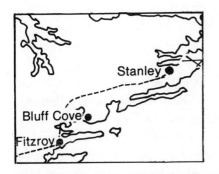

3
Operacion Rosario

On 28 March 1982, two Argentine naval task forces departed the main Argentine naval base at Puerto Belgrano, 300 miles south of Buenos Aires, ostensibly to participate in exercises with the Uruguayan navy. The carrier force (Task Force 20), was comprised of the small (light) aircraft carrier *25 de Mayo* (flag); destroyers *Segui, Comodoro Py, Piedrabuena* and *Bouchard*; oiler *Punta Medanos*; and tug *Sobral*. An amphibious task force (TF 40) included destroyers *Santisima Trinidad* (flag) and *Hercules*; corvettes *Drummond* and *Granville*; the landing ship *Cabo San Antonio*; the submarine *Santa Fe*; two transports, carrying the 2nd Marine Battalion (reinforced), and other units.

This fleet included the two new British–designed Type 42 destroyers *Hercules* and *Santisima Trinidad*; and two of the three equally new French-built A-69 corvettes, *Drummond* and *Granville* (*Guerrico* being the third). There was as centerpiece Argentina's only aircraft carrier, an ex-British light carrier. All the other surface combatants carried missiles and modern electronics, including the latest radars, the other (ex-U.S. World War II) ships having been updated over the years. Together they represented close to a maximum Argentine naval effort.

Instead of steaming north, as they should, however, the two-force fleet sailed southeast. *Operacion Rosario*, the recapture of the

Falklands, had probably been worked on by every rising naval staff officer for years. This reportedly included then Captain Jorge Isaac Anaya, in the late 1960s. It had now begun.

The previous weekend, naval leaves had suddenly been cancelled. Equipment and stores were rushed to Puerto Belgrano and to Comodore Rivadavia, the largest naval airbase convenient to the Falklands. Overflights of Stanley by Argentine aircraft became frequent (a C-130 transport had actually made an "emergency" landing there on 11 March).

Men from all three Argentine armed services would take part in the coming operations, but for obvious reasons it was the navy that would have the greater role. Command reflected this. Admiral Isaac Anaya was now commander-in-chief of the navy, representing naval interests on the ruling junta as well as allocating resources and overseeing operations. Rear Admiral Jose Lombardo was CTF 20, Rear Admiral Gualter Allara CTF 40. Rear Admiral Carlos Busser commanded the landing force.

Argentine rules of engagement stipulated that the occupation was as far as possible to be carried out without inflicting any losses on the British, either human or material. This was recognized as being of considerable political importance, affecting both future relations with the islanders and eventual settlement with the British.

Simultaneously, Task Force 60 formed by the polar transport *Bahia Paraiso* with her marines and the corvette *Guerrico* and led by Captain C. Trombeta (Commander, Naval Antarctic Group) was ordered to occupy Grytviken and Leith on South Georgia. This would complete seizure of the long contested island chain.

This somehow was not quite the best time for the Argentines to initiate any large scale naval operation. On their side, they were simply unprepared for a sudden escalation of the dispute. *Bahia Buen Suceso* (a naval transport) originally was on a commercial voyage working for the salvors. *Bahia Paraiso* was on an Antarctic expedition. A number of ships important to this operation were under repair and refit. The new Super Extendard/Exocet-equipped naval air squadron—slated to become a key equalizer in any armed conflict with the British—was not yet either completely equipped or manned. More new destroyers, frigates, and submarines were on order and due to begin arriving shortly, adding significantly to the fleet.

On the other hand, British station ship *Endurance*—due to be withdrawn shortly and not replaced—had evidently not yet actually been pulled out. The Royal Marine detachment was in the process of turning over to a relief; both old and new units were present, temporarily doubling the men. The Argentine national airline (LADE) maintained an office in Stanley, and Argentine intelligence must have known all this.

But there may not have been a lot of choice. Newswires arriving in Buenos Aires indicated that London was sending three more Royal Navy ships south in reaction to the trouble mounting there. These appeared to include the nuclear-powered attack submarine *Superb* from Gibraltar, the destroyer *Exeter* from the Caribbean, and an unidentified oiler. This news may actually have helped force the Argentine ruling junta's hand.

On 2 April, 1982 Argentina seized from Great Britain the Falkland Islands (called by them the Malvinas), 400 miles off their southeastern coast, and on the next day took South Georgia (Georgias del Sur), 800 miles farther to the southeast, as if reading from a script. Only token resistance was offered by the defenders, the 90 man detachment of Royal Marines (70 on East Falkland, 20 on South Georgia), against what had to be a carefully studied, well-planned and long prepared move.

On the evening of 28 March, off the Falklands, Task Force 20 had separated from the others, steaming to take position about 450 miles north of the Malvinas. TF 20's *25 de Mayo* thus formed the core of a force covering the operation against outside interference, especially from the north. For this task she had embarked an air group of four S-2s, eight A-4s, and some helicopters.

TF 40, built around the landing ship *Cabo San Antonio* and the other transports, meanwhile ran into difficulties. By midday of 29 March, still steaming southeast, Task Force 40 found hard going, facing 40 knot winds and heavy seas, suffering some weather damage.

On 30 March the planned amphibious landing was delayed until 2 April. The task force reduced speed and moved into the lee of the islands to reduce the pounding its ships were taking and to give the seasick troops a chance to get back on their feet. On 2 April, TF 40 executed a full-scale assault on the Stanley area, putting ashore some 1,000 men. In what can best be described as a deliberate display of overwhelming strength (*force majeure*), at dawn Argentine advance parties that had begun landing clandestinely the previous evening rounded up the British marines (unfortunately allowing press photographs of the marine prisoners spreadeagled on the ground), seized the governor, and secured Stanley airport, six miles from town. The bulk of TF 40's landing force then began pouring ashore from landing craft and tracked vehicles. They were supported by Argentina's only aircraft carrier, its only really operational six destroyers, and other ships. They quickly overcame the small Royal Marine detachment. At 0915, bowing to the inevitable, the Queen's governor surrendered the islands.

The next day on South Georgia, after a sharp little fight, the Argentine navy collected the 20 man party of Royal Marines. Small groups of Argentine marines were then stationed at Grytviken and Leith as a symbol of Argentine rights on these lands. It was all very neatly done. There were no British and very few Argentine losses.

At Puerto Argentino (Stanley) an alien flag was raised over an occupied people. Destroyer *Hercules* temporarily assumed air control in the area, including approach and access to the airport. An Argentine military governor assumed responsibility, and the garrison settled in. Army units which had been flown in on air force C-130s were moved by ship to occupying positions at Goose Green/Darwin and Fox Bay. The navy left a group forming the Malvinas Naval Station and the Aeronaval Station as well as elements of the 2nd Marine Battalion in the area. British prisoners and any islanders who wished to accompany them were quietly returned home via Uruguay. Task Force 40 was dissolved.

But it began to appear that the British would counter force with force. The Malvinas were within range of sufficient Argentine air cover and conceivably could be held, although the same did not hold true for the Georgias. Argentina, therefore, now proceded to massively reinforce the occupying troops on the Malvinas by sea and air until they eventually totaled some 12,000 officers and men of all services and arms. Auxiliary airstrips were developed at Goose Green and Pebble Island.

On 8, 9, and 13 April, naval units *Cabo San Antonio, Bahia Buen Suceso*; coastguard patrol vessels *Rio Iguazu* and *Islas Malvinas*; and merchant vessels *Formosa* and *Rio Carcarana* successfully landed further equipment, supplies, and troops at Puerto Argentino. Little arrived by sea after that.

The Argentine navy initiated its own operational developments to support its role in any extended defense of the Malvinas. Transports *Bahia Paraiso* and *Isla de los Estados,* an assortment of naval aircraft, the two coastguard patrol vessels and helicopters, more marines (The 2nd Marine Battalion's party was relieved by the whole 5th Battalion) and combat support units were sent out.

The Georgias were beyond sufficient Argentine air cover and it was recognized that they could not really be held. However, the original token marine garrison was left in place.

Just in case, the navy's unready French-built Super Etendard-equipped 2nd Aeronaval Squadron was ordered to complete its operational readiness, prepared to employ its air-to-surface Exocet missibles in combat. On a crash basis, it developed a flight profile enabling it to operate against an enemy 400–500 miles away. This profile specifically included airborne refueling. Cooperating P-2 maritime patrol aircraft were to provide necessary reconnaissance, helping conserve the Etendard's fuel. Attacks were to be by pairs. Entry into the launch area was to be low, as discreet as circumstances permitted, launching as rapid as possible, and escape as fast as one could go. Stanley airfield could be used only by planes in trouble.

Argentina also converted icebreaker *Almirante Irizar* and supply ship *Bahia Paraiso* into hospital ships. These ships steamed regularly between the Malvinas and the mainland.

At this point, things looked pretty grim. The Malvinas were obviously going to be the center of a major air-sea battle. The dispatch boats *Alferez Sobral* and *Comodoro Somellera* were stationed off the islands for search and rescue, a harbinger of difficult days to come. Argentine success had yet to be paid for, and it was becoming increasingly probable that some price beyond the token already given would have to be paid. Rear Admiral Eduardo Otero became Commander, Naval Forces Malvinas.

THE STRATEGIC CALCULATION

If the Argentine military junta in the Casa Rosada (Buenos Aires) had had their political radar turned on in recent years—and they undoubtedly did—they could not but have received certain encouraging politico-military signals. Those must have served to indicate a significant diminishing of British interest in projecting its power anywhere overseas, much less in these remote islands:

- The Royal Navy had been steadily reduced in strength by every recent administration to the point where it apparently would be hard pressed only to defend its home shores and fulfill its NATO commitments;
- A significant proportion of the Royal Navy was devoted to maintenance of a Polaris submarine-based strategic nuclear deterrent, soon to be replaced by Trident missile submarines;
- The whole Trident ballistic submarine program was to be paid for out of current navy funds, ensuring a further steady reduction in the surface fleet;
- *Eagle* and *Ark Royal,* both conventional (medium) aircraft carriers of 50,000 tons, were broken up without replacement;
- The Fleet Air Arm had turned its F-4 fighters over to the Royal Air Force and scrapped its fighter direction aircraft, leaving only VSTOL and helicopters, nothing to provide really adequate cover for operations in a hostile air environment in distant waters;
- Of the remaining two operational British aircraft carriers—once conventional now VSTOL *Hermes* (24,000 tons) and brand new small VSTOL carrier *Invincible* (16,000 tons)—*Hermes* was soon to be retired and *Invincible,* the first of a class of three, was to be sold, leaving a planned future total of only two carriers, both VSTOL;

- In 1967 the British had as a matter of official defense policy public-ly renounced the landing or withdrawal of troops against sophisticated opposition outside the range of land-based air cover;
- Britain's only two amphibious assault ships (*Fearless* and *Intrepid*, both of 12,000 tons) were listed for disposal; destroying *Intrepid* had already begun;
- Commando carrier *Bulwark* (23,300 tons) was retired early, and her scrapping swifty approved;
- The first batches of the new Type 22 missile frigates (the 3,500 ton *Broadswords*) carried no large caliber gun, leaving them lit-tle capability for amphibious support;
- Chatham base was due to be closed and Portsmouth Dockyard allowed to run down;
- *Triumph* (17,500 tons), heavy fleet repair ship, a perhaps unromantic type absolutely necessary to suggest any extended large scale distant operation, was scrapped; and finally,
- *Endurance* (3,600 tons), an ice patrol vessel, Britain's sole stand-ing naval presence in the far South Atlantic and South Polar seas area, was being withdrawn without replacement, and from then on, there would only be occasional visits.

In a dangerous, unstable world, the Queen's distant posses-sions must have looked very exposed indeed. The British could not have been very interested in any longer defending them by military means. Or so it seemed.

Once mighty Britain depended in the coming crisis primarily on a then too small, still shrinking, but superb Royal Navy, oriented primarily toward North Atlantic ASW and strategic deterrence. The Royal Navy had already shrunk to two small aircraft carriers, 63 destroyers and frigates, 12 nuclear-powered attack submarines, 16 conventional submarines, and four Polaris-armed missile sub-marines. As it turned out, two amphibious assault ships and six landing ships were still available, more or less. Its capability for set piece sea battles, amphibious landings, and naval gunfire sup-port—three out of five of the textbook components of sea power*—

---

*The other two being here considered large scale convoys and related ASW, and submarine warfare.

were, however, either going or already gone. The navy was supported as much as possible by a professional RAF and army, themselves heavily committed to NATO.

Of perhaps more immediate interest to the junta here was one last fact: both of the remaining operational British aircraft carriers—*Hermes* and *Invincible*—were at the moment in Portsmouth Dockyard. A number of other significant warships were also undergoing routine refit or in various states of reduced readiness.

Operacion Rosario may have had to be sprung a little early, but it was due sooner or later, and it was probably a relief to have it over. Execution at this point may have actually been for the best. Militarily there might not ever really be a better time. Overall, the Argentines enjoyed quantitative superiority in the air, in some other areas a qualitative one (better equipment), and at the start, all the strategic advantages of being the ones already there. If possession is nine-tenths of the law, the junta was finally in glorious, heady possession. The British would now have to come to them. *Rosario* was allowed to stand. Intense preparations for a defence were put in train.

The Argentines relied heavily on a 230 plane, modern, well-balanced, and well-trained air force (some of whose pilots were trained in the United States and Israel) to counter Britain's navy, help break any blockade, and support their largely conscript army as well as their navy. Their navy was typically that of a significant regional power. It was even smaller than Britain's (they had only a single carrier), ageing, mostly second hand, but balanced, untypically good, and modernizing slowly.

While the total balance of purely naval forces appeared in this instance to give an overwhelming superiority to the Royal Navy, the Argentine junta obviously calculated that in the context of its European commitment (NATO) only a fraction of Britain's available forces would be spared for the South Atlantic, to counter any junta move. It did not much matter, in any event. There Argentina could bring its air power to bear. American leaders had reckoned similarly for a century and a half.

Two first class adversaries thus faced off in the Falklands. Overall, on the ground they should have been about equal in strength; but on top of everything else the British were forced to operate 8,000 miles from home while the Argentines were right next door. All in all, the Argentine seizure seemed a safe move. A serious British reaction was "scarcely possible" and "totally improbable," as one Argentine leader put it. The expectation seems to have been on a British demonstration of force, followed by negotiations to regularize what had already been done. Aside from saving face, then, the Royal Navy's main function would seemingly be limited to strengthening London's negotiating position.

Argentina's relations with Chile have seldom been good. This could have provided a damping on Argentine ambitions. Relations were at the moment being exacerbated by a dispute over three small islands in Beagle Channel, south of the Strait of Magellan. Concerned that Argentina would continue on against them, the Chilean navy had already sailed south, concentrating its base at Punta Arenas. Chile, however, posed little if any present armed threat; its armed forces were starved of modern equipment by a human rights embargo. Its restraining effect here was almost nil.

Argentina's relations with the United States had been improving. The Casa Rosada had been helping with counterinsurgency in Central America, and its human rights troubles at home seemed to be easing off. The junta seems to have counted on our neutrality in what was to come.

The violent far South Atlantic winter was coming on, bringing with it a continuous succession of notoriously severe Antarctic storms and nights 15 hours long. Icebergs, frequent gale-force winds, ice, sleet, snow, fog, heavy rain, and subfreezing cold would be the order of the day. Thirty to 40 foot seas are common. Wind-chill could be very dangerous. Flying would be difficult, ASW a nightmare. Once the Argentines were in place in the islands, the coming winter would be on their side. Any British naval reaction would be unlikely until spring, if ever. All this fine weather—much like the Shetlands in winter—was only weeks away (due mid-June), and must have formed part of Argentine calculations.

Not taken into account in Argentina's strategic estimate were the political, social, and moral factors that would become involved in any military confrontation. Buenos Aires had "illegally" and openly seized the islands by force. The islanders did not want to become Argentine and said so. Here was no government by consent. These are intangibles, and the omission is perhaps a natural one for a ruling junta made up of generals and admirals. For this mistake they would pay.

Foremost among the omissions in the Argentine thought process must have been the almost universal outrage expressed by individual Britons over Argentina's seizure of the islands. After decades of political frustration and surrender of one colony after another, this loss was just one too many. United for the first time in many years, the British rose almost as a single people in support of their government.

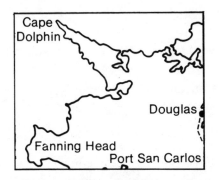

4
Task Force South

To the surprise of many, Her Majesty's Government announced (3 April) and immediately (4 April) began to assemble, the first of a fleet (properly, a task oriented Task Force made up from units of The Fleet) and to charter/requisition merchant ships. On 5 April the lead echelon of this fleet was dispatched to the Falklands area. As the government began making warlike noises, the fleet was steadily built up.

Argentine seizure of the islands had pulled many of the levers of the subconscious British tribal memory. Involved here were such things as defense of a small and distant colony, protection of the rights and persons of Englishmen abroad, and maintenance of the honor of their flag all rolled into one. "Aggression must not be allowed to succeed," declared Prime Minister Margaret Thatcher in words that came from and echoed far down British military and imperial history.

Fortunately, from the politico-military viewpoints, Britain was free to act alone, and at once. Access to the Falklands needed no overflight rights from third countries, nor were there any maritime choke points through which the ships had to pass and that could be diplomatically or militarily closed off. The route south lay entirely on or over the high seas, waters politically neutral if sometimes environmentally hostile and always seemingly endless.

Actually the Admiralty does not seem to have been caught entirely short. British intelligence had already alerted them to a number of possible Argentine navy-related actions. A wide range of options open to Buenos Aires were listed:

1. harassment of foreign (third party) trawlers using Port Stanley;
2. a landing on South Georgia;
3. private ("free lance") landings on the main islands;
4. occupation of an uninhabited island;
5. a full scale invasion.

Planning for a Falklands naval force had begun sometime as early as mid to late March, when as a counter to a reported Argentine naval presence in Falklands waters, a task group of some three destroyers/frigates was first alerted to sail for the South Atlantic. On 1 April as the situation worsened, plans were drawn up to prepare a larger force, now including small aircraft carrier *Invincible* and perhaps six other warships. On 2 April these plans were expanded again. An oiler had already been sent on ahead, ready to fuel whatever came.

The Royal Navy was going to need all the ships it could get. Ships under repair or refit were rushed out of the yards. Those in reserve were hurriedly brought out.* Those on the disposal/sale list that could be useful were recommissioned. At least one already sold was called back. They were all fueled, stored and ammunitioned, and made ready for sea.

Men poured into the ships and units. They came back from leave, alerted by signs at railway stations, telegrams, phone calls or were transferred. Selected reservists were called up.

Portsmouth is an old navy port. It had seen essentially the same scene played out time and time again over the centuries. On 5 April *Hermes* and *Invincible,* their decks lined with Sea Harriers

---

*The navy was able to substitute ships from its stand-by squadron at Chatham—principally elderly frigates—for some that had to be taken off NATO tasks.

and Sea King helicopters weighed anchor, exchanged courtesies with HMS *Victory*, and headed down the Solent on the morning tide. Once out in the English Channel, the ships were joined by escorts and others from Plymouth (Devonport) and ports elsewhere, until once past Gibraltar a 28 ship fleet had been gathered, including Britain's entire carrier force. They then headed southwest into the Atlantic, into the sharp wind and grey swell of the Western Approaches. The ships were cheered as they left. There were as usual also some tears shed.

Assault ship HMS *Fearless* left the next day, putting on a little show as she went. She was followed out of harbor by her four embarked utility landing craft (LCUs). Once off the Isle of Wight, the ship lowered her stern, flooded her after well, took in the four LCUs, and continued on her way.

The navy must at first have expected and much preferred even what might be considered the classic doctrinal sequence of maritime related events now to take place. Such a sequence would encompass an unavoidably long approach by the fleet to the Falklands; local maneuvering for position; perhaps a naval demonstration; and finally a large air and sea battle between themselves and the Argentines to gain command of the immediate sea area and to break the Argentine blockade assumed to be in place by then.

Doctrine said that unless peace broke out along the way, the British would absolutely have to meet and destroy the enemy fleet, or at least drive it back into its bases. This battle the British would have to be ready to fight and win.

Doctrine emphasized that the primary concern of a fleet commander in such a situation must be to establish air superiority over his task force, and then over the objective area. This is usually accomplished first with combat air patrols (CAPs) over the fleet, and then with offensive sorties against enemy air formations and their supporting facilities (airfields, aircraft carriers, ground control). During a successful amphibious landing, the beachhead must be isolated and then defended in a similar way.

This was also a classic set up for a naval blockade. Ships could seal off the islands on and under the sea, later adding an air quarantine and an electronic blockade by jamming. Cut off from their base, the Argentine occupiers could be softened up at leisure either for a diplomatic solution or eventual physical eviction.

Subsequently maintaining British control with but a small fraction of their force, the command just gained would therefore next be exploited by a full naval blockade of their own; then and only then would an amphibious assault be mounted to retake the islands, should that still be called for. The navy prepared accordingly, very efficiently and with amazing speed.

The fleet steamed south. Soon the waters turned bluer, calmer, and sunnier. There was a stop at Ascension. By the Roaring Forties the seas became grey and rough again, the cold winds whipping up the waves, as the fleet gradually began to realize it was really going to war.

The British government ultimately assembled off the Falklands proper a probable 60–70 ships of all kinds: two small VSTOL aircraft carriers, destroyers, frigates, submarines, minesweepers, troopers, assault transports, two additional improvised auxiliary carriers, hospital ships, and a converted landing ship. Antarctic support ship *Endurance* was also still on scene. Bringing along a large fleet train of oilers, replenishment ships, tugs, and merchant cargo vessels of all types, they obviously meant to stay as long as need be.

The force collected for the Falklands operation—what was to be first an opposed blockade and then amphibious assault—must be recognized as a microequivalent of the current Soviet navy, thus willy nilly reflecting its operational philosophy. There were no super attack aircraft carriers and no supersonic air superiority fighters, only small VSTOL carriers, Harriers, and helicopters. Primary reliance in air defense was placed on a variety of surface-to-air missiles, long the Soviet approach, and to a lesser extent on the Harrier VSTOL attack plane. The amphibious group was a scratch collection of mostly merchant vessels, with two assault ships.

There was of necessity a heavy reliance on and integration of requisitioned and chartered merchantmen to augment and support regular British naval vessels. *Atlantic Conveyor,* a 17,000 ton combination ro-ro and container ship, was Arapahoed and utilized as an aircraft ferry, taking on five RAF Harriers and a number of helicopters. *Atlantic Causeway,* her sister, was similarly Arapahoed, and was employed as an ASW carrier, embarking ten Sea King helicopters. *Queen Elizabeth 2* and *Canberra* became troop transports. *Uganda* was converted into a hospital ship. *Elk,* a ro-ro ferry, carried heavy engineering equipment, ammunition and tanks. Five fishing trawlers became minesweepers. This, too, is standard Soviet practice.

In expectation of a requirement for additional naval air assets, four new naval air squadrons (one of Sea Harriers, two of Wessex helicopters, and one of Sea Kings) were formed. In addition, several new small flights, consisting mainly of Wasp helos (helicopters), were prepared for the ships taken up from trade and warships taken from the sales/disposal list.

Considerably assisting the navy in its own mobilization was the happy accident of having some of its ships already at top line, at Gibraltar for exercises (NATO's "Spring Train") in the Mediterranean. The navy was further aided in calling up the merchantmen by extensive NATO plans completed earlier. Everything useful was drawn in. There was remarkably little administrative fuss.

The Royal Air Force (RAF) made strenuous efforts to be counted in the battle. Individual Vulcan heavy bombers fueled by Victor long range tankers, both flying via Ascension Island, made several runs on Port Stanley's small airfield. RAF Harriers (GR3s) and helicopters operated from *Atlantic Conveyor.* The Harriers appear to have made it ashore before *Conveyor* was sunk, and continued to fly from there. More RAF Harriers arrived directly from Britain, via Ascension, refueling air-to-air en route. RAF Nimrods, operating out of Ascension deep into the South Atlantic, provided maritime reconnaissance and ASW capability. But it was always the Royal Navy's show.

Ro-ro: *Roll on, roll on.*

Arapahod: *Arbitrary name for system whereby merchantmen are fitted with helicopters and/or VSTOL aircraft.*

Once again the British army (together with Royal Marine commandos) was employed as "a projectile to be fired by the navy." The navy swiftly loaded first one brigade, then another (some 9,000 picked troops, not anywhere near the three to one theoretically necessary to turf out the foe), rapidly lifted them 8,000 miles, landed them successfully, supported them, supplied them, and saw them to victory. The traditional role of both services was played to the full and, despite considerable improvisation, the system worked with never a serious hitch. The navy's institutional memory did not fail it.

British power was in the end actually applied to the Falklands problem in six natural and graduated phases, each signalling resolve, blending into and continuing with the next phase: (1) advance into the South Atlantic; (2) blockade and isolation; (3) reconnaissance; (4) recapture of South Georgia; (5) raids on the Falklands by commandos and aircraft; and (6) recapture of the Falklands. No more force was ever applied than proved necessary, as could best be judged at the time. The Argentines could have evacuated at any time in good order and with dignity; that option was always kept open for them. Their military humiliation was never the aim. The Argentine fleet was never met.

Britain—and perhaps Argentina—had a nuclear capability, although only Britain had organized delivery systems. Nuclear weapons played no part either in assessments of the local balance of military strength or in the British concept of operations. The perceived interests on either side clearly did not warrant their use. It was conventional forces that would determine the outcome of the coming battle.

In these militarily ill-balanced circumstances, air cover for the British fleet could never be complete, the blockade never firmly in place. It was also clear that both sides here could hurt each other badly. The battle for the Falklands could be a long one. With orders to be as quick as possible, the Royal Navy prepared for the worst. Some still did not believe it would actually come to hostilities.

COMMAND AND CONTROL

In the Falklands we were given only fragmentary glimpses of the working British command, control, communications, and intelligence set up. The higher management of the crisis was conducted in London at cabinet level by a small group of the most concerned ministers, chaired by the Prime Minister, meeting almost daily. The government's principal military advisor, Chief of the Defence Staff, was naturally in attendance. This group ensured that the diplomatic, economic, and military aspects of policy were coordinated. Of course, the government set the mission and approved the rules of engagement. It established the guidelines within which commanders were to operate, without making any attempt to fight the battle from 8,000 miles away.

General operational timing was, as could be expected, reserved for the highest political decision, releases being given at least for actually opening hostilities and then both for the initial landing and for the final assault on Port Stanley.

Once it had approved the commanders' general war plan, however, the government was said to have issued not a single operational order. Supposedly, neither did Downing Street offer any military advice. Specific timing was left to the operational commanders, tactical considerations, and the weather. At least in general, this seems to have been true.

At the Ministry of Defence, Admiral of the Fleet Sir Terence Lewin trod the corridors of power as Chief of the Defence Staff. It was he who daily dealt with the cabinet group and who ensured that the navy was left to run the operation without unwanted outside help. Admiral Sir Henry Leach held the post of First Sea Lord at what remained of the Admiralty. The navy was well represented in higher circles. The navy presented the dispatch of the task force as a strictly senior service affair; it was a conventional naval deterrent in support of diplomacy. Mobilization of warships, merchant ships and marines was its business. The other services were only to lend necessary support. Fighting changed little.

Overall military command and coordination of the Falklands operation was exercised by Commander in Chief Fleet (Admiral Sir John Fieldhouse) as Commander Task Force 317, a triservice force (all surface ships, land, and air components), and CTF 324 (the submarines). His mission was to conduct military deployments and order operations to repel an attack on British people and territory, to support the withdrawal of Argentine forces from the Falklands and the dependencies, and to reestablish British administration there as quickly as possible. He reported operationally direct to Admiral Lewin.

Although reportedly neither the Ministry of Defence (the Admiralty, Whitehall in London) nor Headquarters Commander in Chief Fleet (Northwood, outside London) exercised direct tactical control over the Falklands task force, they did provide strategic and logistic support. They identified, assembled, forwarded, and updated the necessary resources. They exercised at least a watching brief over tactics. Reportedly, at the last minute, they provided from their staff the landing force commander and flew him out.

Most of the overall strategic and operational decisions were thus made at the cabinet-Lewin level, logistic decisions at the Ministry of Defence (MoD). These decisions went for execution to the unflappable Commander in Chief Fleet ("Fleet" as he was known) at the navy's underground operational headquarters in Northwood. It was from there that all communications went out to the task force at sea.

Rear Admiral J. F. ("Sandy") Woodward RN, Flag Officer First Flotilla, a former staff officer (Director of Naval Plans) at the Admiralty, was on-scene commander (Commander of the Task Groups), exercising effective tactical command of the task force. Major General Jeremy Moore RM led the landing force. Reportedly their only instructions were that the islands be quickly retaken, casualties be kept to a minimum, and that there be no bombing of Argentine mainland airbases or, probably, mining of harbors. These officers were carefully chosen, one can be sure. Not only Nelson and St. Vincent, Rodney and Collingwood, but the whole world was watching them.

Carriers *Hermes* and *Invincible* both would have to go, obviously. So would both *Fearless* and *Intrepid*. The force would also require escorts. Taking part in the NATO exercises at Gilbraltar were three modern general purpose destroyers—Type 42s *Coventry, Glasgow,* and *Sheffield,* armed with Sea Dart. Also there were two ready Type 22s *Broadsword* and *Brilliant* carrying Seawolf, frigates critical to the force's air defense. Beyond these, the force would simply be given all the destroyers and frigates that could be found.

Although information on British fleet organization is spotty, one final logical task oriented breakdown of the Falklands force could have been as follows:

FALKLAND ISLANDS TASK FORCE (TF 317):

- carrier battle group (including *Hermes,* fleet flagship)
- amphibious task group (*Fearless,* flagship)
- landing group (the marine and army landing force)
- South Georgia group (mixed, one-shot)
- South Sandwich group (mixed, one-shot)
- picket group
- escort group(s)
- RAF group
- fleet train
- fleet base(s)

The submarines, with less directly related tasks and different methods, were kept autonomous, formed into a task force of their own (TF 324). Their operations were integrated at Northwood, and of course Woodward was kept closely in touch with what they were doing.

Task groups were created and disestablished as necessity dictated; units were transferred to and between them the same way. This organization does conform with what is known from the press. It is a standard one. The concept at least should be valid.

Since their Harriers were indispensable for air superiority missions (there was nothing else), ground attack and ad hoc combat air patrol, and their helicopters for ASW, the only two operational regular British carriers—*Hermes* and *Invincible*—constituted the key to the offensive. Initially they were to gain local command of the sea, then support whatever came next. If the Argentines sank or even just disabled them, the campaign would be over. They were formed into a single carrier task ("battle") group.

The carrier group shifted from an administrative into a combat formation as it moved south through the Roaring Forties. Three destroyers or frigates led the way, in line, some 20 miles ahead. In the center of a defensive close screen came the two priceless carriers, escorted for the moment by *Broadsword* and *Brilliant,* armed with antimissile missiles and accompanied by the oiler. The carriers seem to have moved and fought essentially as a unit, *Invincible* with its better radar (and fewer planes) assuming basic responsibility for air defense, *Hermes* taking on that for offensive strikes.

Ordinarily kept well to the east and northeast of the islands where they were beyond the effective range of most Argentine combat aircraft, the carriers were committed inside Argentine range only when absolutely necessary, and then for the minimum of time. While necessary, such tactics considerably lessened their ability to provide continuous air cover to other elements of the task force.

The carriers' Sea Harriers were utilized throughout by the force for combat air patrol (CAP), reconnaissance, and strike (especially ground attack and radar suppression). They operated from beginning to end under the full command and control of Admiral Woodward. Sea Harriers typically flew CAP in pairs, orbiting at medium height north of Pebble Island, west of West Falkland, and over the southern entrance to Falkland Sound.

Up until the beachhead was established, the RAF Harriers flew under the control of Admiral Woodward, during which time Stanley airfield and the various air strips were their principal targets. Later in the campaign, after the British strip was established ashore, these GR3s were tasked under the direction of the Commander, Land Forces. This utilized the skills of the RAF pilots in their usual reconnaissance, ground attack, and close air support role, in conjunction with forward air controllers on the front line.

As the task force neared the South Atlantic and came within submarine range of Argentine bases, Sea King helicopters, armed with dipping sonars, ASW torpedoes, and depth charges, began their endless ASW patrols around the ships. The helos were also prepared to provide over the horizon guidance for surface-to-surface missiles fired from the ships.

In the closing days, Sea Kings hovered close to high value British ships at the estimated flight height of an Exocet (five to six feet above the water). If an incoming missile was sighted, the agile decoy, having attracted it, was to jink violently out of the way. The

Exocet in theory would be unable to follow the maneuver and would pass harmlessly by.

If accomplishing their mission meant digging the enemy out of the islands with the bayonet, the British were prepared for that, too. Even the names of the infantry regiments making up the landing force—Parachute, Welsh and Scots Guards, and Gurkha—as well as the commandoes and other special units, evoked memories of great deeds. These all were organized basically into two reinforced brigades (3 Commando and 5 Infantry), each major trooper conveniently carrying one.

Following standard amphibious doctrine, once a significant fraction of the landing force was successfully ashore, troop command was transferred ashore. Once it was large and balanced enough to be self-sustaining and was so recognized by both navy task force and landing force commanders the landing force of two brigades plus metamorphosed into Land Forces Falkland Islands, a command organization in its own right.

Few expeditionary forces have faced and overcome such difficult problems of command and control. Its units came from all three services, gathered from far and near. They were scattered for much of the time en route over thousands of square miles of sea. Admiral Woodward used helicopters to bring his subordinates to him in *Hermes* for important conferences and staff meetings, but there was no way of producing any practised command structured in the time allowed. This speaks wonders for the military school system, which gave everyone the same overall conceptual frame.

The landing force was distributed among a number of ships arriving in the area at different times. This makes all the more remarkable the landing of an integrated force at San Carlos. Most troops had never seen their landing force or even brigade commander before then. Organizational cohesiveness, only theoretically in existence on departure from Britain, was developed at sea and worked efficiently on land. That speaks wonders for leadership at all levels.

Intelligence of the enemy almost certainly proved to be a major problem for both sides. At times in the early stages it seemed that both sides were playing blind man's bluff. Finding the operational intelligence provided by surface vessels, Harriers, and helicopters insufficient, the British reacted with characteristic energy. They brought in Nimrods for long range surveillance and reconnaissance. They may have been getting some satellite data from the United States under longstanding agreements. They must have exploited their submarines at least in part here. Radio interception was obviously used, as was radio direction finding and code breaking. The British landed small observer teams on both the mainland and the islands, and in the islands, they raided. Evidently, it was enough finally. But that was not all intelligence did.

To help exploit the element of surprise and to establish British psychological ascendancy, they developed a many-faceted cover and deception plan. Aimed at exaggerating their own strength, playing down their weaknesses, encouraging misleading assumptions as to their plans, and instilling fear among the Argentines, the press was denied significant facts and on occasion was purposefully misled. The government never outright lied, but aircraft, ship, and troop numbers were inflated, the professionalism of the troops stressed. Censorship was rigorous, and on occasion news was held up. Some of this plan was orchestrated in London. Other aspects were improvised on the spot.

Throughout these operations, one continuous input to the British tactical calculation had to be consideration for the local population for whom in large measure this campaign was being fought. Rules of engagement had to allow for the islanders' safety. *Bahia Buen Suceso*, an Argentine blockade runner, escaped being sunk from the air once because she was tied up to a pier in the middle of a settlement. At the end, a no-fire area had to be declared in Stanley, within which the kelpers could take refuge.

The British concept of action was good, sound military stuff, well-practiced over the years. Command and control was first rate, the British somehow managing to avoid having too much of it in spite of a seemingly top-heavy staff. Still not everything went quite as expected. Wars just do not work out that way. The larger elements of their plan were carried through, and that was what was going to matter most.

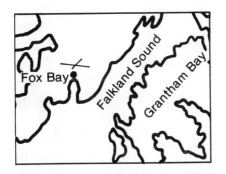

5

Operation Corporate

Her Majesty's Government immediately severed diplomatic relations with Argentina and froze Argentine assets. A complaint was lodged with the United Nations Security Council. The Council passed Resolution 502, condemning the aggression, calling for an immediate withdrawal and a return to negotiation. All ten members of the EEC voted unanimously to impose economic sanctions on Argentina, and to ban the delivery of military equipment and spare parts to the junta.

It is important in what follows to keep in mind that Britain's naval effort was only part of a larger continuing politico-military campaign, the object of which was to ensure that Argentina complied with U.N. Resolution 502 and withdrew her troops from the Falklands, preliminary to further discussions regarding the future of the islands. Britain's strategy concentrated on three areas: (1) diplomacy (through the United Nations); (2) economic sanctions (through the EEC); and (3) force, or blockade with the option of a landing, if necessary.

Drawing strength from years of Admiralty, the British government almost immediately (first on 8 April, to become partially effective 12 April, restated and expanded on 28 April, to take effect 30 April) announced first a "maritime" then a "total" exclusion zone (TEZ). Any ship or aircraft found within 200 nautical miles of the

Falkland Islands without due authority of the Ministry of Defence in London would be considered hostile and liable to attack by British forces. Drawn from the center of the islands, the TEZ could better have been skewed to the east, to give the fleet more maneuver room, but it was not. On 7 May the Admiralty extended this to regard any Argentine warship found more than 12 nautical miles from the Argentine coast as hostile, to be dealt with accordingly. They had earlier also declared a 200 mile defensive envelope around all units of their task force, wherever it might be, warning that any approach by the Argentines that could pose a threat of interference would be dealt with, and that all shadowing vessels would be liable to attack.

The lead element of the fleet took some three weeks, with an approximate speed of advance (SOA) at 15 knots, to reach the Falklands. Picking up the additional units from Gibraltar as it passed, it headed first for Ascension Island. Its time en route was largely spent with planning, organizing, reorganizing, and training. During the interim, there were weeks of intense but fruitless diplomatic negotiations at various levels.

As it was sorted into its various fighting and support elements and formed up at Ascension, the fleet began to assume a recognizable shape. From Ascension, the lead element comprised the principal fighting units of the force—the carrier group. It departed south on 16 April, to attempt to establish air and sea superiority before the more vulnerable amphibious and support groups followed. Argentine long range reconnaissance picked them up on 21 April, 1,600 miles east-northeast of Rio de Janeiro. The fleet continued to build up, as the additional units were made ready and sent on.

The Argentinian government likewise prohibited a 200-mile zone around the Falklands to the British, and assigned a flag officer (apparently Rear Admiral Lombardo) to supervise their blockade effort. This was soon extended to include the entire South Atlantic area. Except for intermittent attempts at enforcement from the air, however, this counterblockade was of little effect.

During the period that Britain's surface fleet steamed so deliberately south, making good only an average 15 knots or so (a "political" speed, perhaps), taking three weeks to make the passage, its Falklands blockade could only be and was theoretically enforced by submarines. The nuclear-powered attack submarines could move at 30 knots, arriving in half the time it took surface ships. At first, they were deployed to cover the approaches to Stanley and the entrances to Falkland Sound, later moving off the mainland coast. It does seem that the Argentines could not have attempted to run very many (if any) merchant ships or major combatants across in this initial period when submarines alone barred their path, or some would have been lost. Again for political reasons (negotiations were still going on), the navy also may have held its fire until the situation could be further defined. In this time the submarines sank no ships, and avoided the stigma of destroying a merchantman with all hands.

On 25 April Britain announced it had recaptured remote, mountainous, and barren South Georgia. South of Ascension a small task group (HMS *Antrim, Plymouth, Brilliant*, and RFA *Tidespring*) had been formed from the main body of the fleet and detached southeast for this purpose, picking up *Endurance* en route. Captain B. G. Young RN commanded the task group.

In addition, *Conqueror* (a nuclear-powered attack submarine) was ordered to patrol also off the islands to prevent any Argentine reinforcement. Maritime patrol aircraft swept the sea areas from South Georgia to the Argentine coast to give early warning of possible hostile naval movements.

A glance at any chart will show that these islands were beyond Argentine air cover. After a short preliminary shelling, British marines were landed by helicopter directly from the ships. They retook Grytviken after a brief exchange of fire with the small Argentine occupying force. Isolated pockets of resistance (Leith) were gradually mopped up. South Georgia immediately provided the fleet with a host of sheltered natural harbors and a welcome uplift to morale. There were no British casualties.

Meanwhile, around the Falklands proper, a number of preliminary British reconnaissance, intelligence gathering, softening up and diversionary operations now began. The British blockade was put into place, as best it could be.

Meanwhile, Argentine jets flew out to probe the task force, to be chased away by the CAP, or in the case of two Mirages and a Canberra, to be shot down. The adversaries were now testing each other.

On 1 May the testing stopped. A large combined air and sea strike hit Stanley airfield and Goose Green. Activities were opened by what may have been the most cost-ineffective operation of the war. A frequently refuelled Vulcan bomber flying from Britain by way of Ascension began the affair by dropping 21 1,000 pound bombs on Stanley field, to little effect. Harriers followed up.

The first major Falklands losses were incurred on both sides in this preliminary blockade stage. On 2 May a British nuclear-powered submarine made the first major kill. *Conqueror* did torpedo and damage the old U.S.-built Argentine cruiser *General Belgrano* (ex-USS *Phoenix*) just off the mainland's southern tip, using conventional torpedoes. *Belgrano*'s two escorting destroyers carried out a highly professional response, but after two nerve-racking hours, *Conqueror* escaped. *Belgrano* subsequently sank. The attack took place outside the British total exclusion zone, and near mainland bases, just outside Argentina's 12 mile limit, but the submarine claimed hot pursuit. (The old U.S.-built Argentine diesel submarine *Santa Fe* had already been sunk. In a totally unrelated action, she was hit and driven ashore by British aircraft during operations at South Georgia, while being used as an emergency transport and supply vessel.) HMS *Sheffield* was hit by a missile while on picket duty on 4 May and eventually sank. This was no longer a show of force.

There is some evidence that Argentine West German-built Type 209 diesel submarines did in this period twice successfully penetrate the British ASW screens, execute attacks on British ships and escape. On 5 May, reportedly, *San Luis* conducted runs against several targets, firing wireguided torpedoes, *Invincible* supposedly being one of the targets. None of the torpedoes fired ever exploded, for unknown reasons. During her escape *San Luis* was tracked by ASW ships and helicopters for approximately 72 hours. The British prosecuted a number of sonar contacts and fired a lot of ASW ordnance. The Argentine returned undamaged to port.

On 9 May two Harriers had located a fishing vessel that was behaving suspiciously and strafed her. The crew surrendered and the vessel, *Narwal,* was boarded from a helicopter. She was found to be an intelligence collector with two naval officers on board and writtten instructions on what to report. *Narwal* later sank while under tow.

In Falkland Sound on 11 May *Alacrity* intercepted the Argentine supply ship *Isla de los Estados* attempting to run the blockade under cover of darkness, in bad weather with low clouds and poor visibility. Located by radar, the Argentine was challenged, refused to heave to, and was hit by gunfire, exploded, and sank. The explosion lit up the sky. *Isla* may have been carrying a cargo of mines or fuel, or both.

Several other Argentine ships (two armed cargo vessels, two naval tugs, a patrol boat or two, and at least one interisland steamer) were also shot up during this time by aircraft and surface ships, both.

As combat wastage inevitably began to mount, Western Europe's ban on arms shipments was bound sooner or later to hurt Argentina badly. Four frigates and a submarine ordered from West Germany were held up. Perhaps of more immediate impact, France forbade several imminent scheduled shipments of aircraft, missiles, ammunition, and spare parts.

The fleet continued to gather. The carrier battle group of some nine ships collected on the northeastern edge of the 200-mile zone, waiting for the others to join them. The large amphibious group was en route. Other ships were still leaving Ascension. A further 11 had sailed from Britain on 10 May. It was to be the largest naval assembly since Suez.

The Argentines had announced that they had mined local waters, and they did in fact lay some moored contact mines in the deep approaches to Stanley and elsewhere. The Royal Navy hurriedly formed a minecountermeasures squadron, consisting of five requisitioned 1,200 ton deep sea fishing trawlers (their trawls easily converted for sweeping) and a mother ship (tender). Four of the trawlers were employed as sweepers, one became a support ship.

Over the Falklands, 400 miles from their mainland bases, Argentine aircraft operated at almost their extreme radius of action. Achievable mission profiles could not allow for extensive searches or long combat. On the other hand, the British carriers had to come within range to launch their shortlegged (100 mile at most radius) Harriers against the islands. The British nonetheless moved aggressively at every point. Where they could, they staged their planes forward.

Although the British never assembled enough air power to establish air superiority of their own over the Falklands, as their Harriers met and knocked Argentine strike aircraft out of the sky, bombed and strafed Argentine island airfields, the British destroyed initial Argentine control of the air. The navy kept at least one Harrier on flight deck alert, pilot strapped in, ready for immediate scramble at all times. The Harriers were soon able to help isolate the islands, and when the time came, to join the ground fight.

While all the more obvious combat activity was taking place, the British were extensively engaged in covert preparations for possible landings. Men of both the Special Air Service (SAS) and Special Boat Service (SBS) had been ashore in South Georgia and the Falklands from as early as 18 April, mainly gathering information. Eventually about 300 of them were operating there in small groups. These were variously landed by helicopter, small boats from surface ships and from *Onyx* (a quiet, diesel-powered submarine).

Time, as it always is in war, was absolutely critical. At home politically, the British had to move before the first flush of popular support evaporated. Abroad they had to complete the operation before world opinion could be mobilized against them, leaving the Argentines in control, or before other powers could become involved. Added to this, the southern winter in an area where it is noted for its ferocity was almost upon them. Troops could not be kept indefinitely on board ship. They would get bored, physically out of condition, and stale. It was move soon or not at all.

During the night of 14–15 May there occurred what may not have been the beginning of the end, but was certainly the end of the beginning. A 120 man Royal Marine/Special Air Service raiding party, under cover of a bombardment by *Glamorgan*, was landed by helicopter on Pebble (Borbon) Island, just west of the northern entrance to Falkland Sound. Before withdrawing, they destroyed a number of aircraft, a large surveillance radar, fuel and ammunition dumps. They were clear by dawn, running at 29 knots into a force nine gale. The way in to the islands was now open.

Everyone waited for the next move. This was an anxious time for Britain's allies. What would happen if the Royal Navy suffered an overwhelming defeat? There was no guarantee that they would not be decimated by the very competent Argentine air force. Would the remnants have to be rescued? By whom? What would this kind of debacle mean for NATO's North Atlantic defenses? Much more than British interests were at risk in those frigid waters.

In April a Dublin (Ireland) bookmaker had offered odds of 6 to 4 against Britain retaking the Falklands within six months. He had plenty of takers. At mid-May, the odds looked to be still about the same.

THE LANDING

Although by mid-May it was plain that some considerable force would probably have to be used to eject the Argentine occupiers, the single best-known example of deliberate British official disinformation occurred at this point. At a 20 May Ministry of Defence briefing, it was stated that British forces were *not* planning a full-scale invasion of the islands, but rather looking to a continuing series of hit and run raids. Even as the briefer (a senior official) spoke (not for attribution, of course) a major amphibious landing, the culmination of "Operation Corporate," was in fact getting under way.

The Argentines had concentrated most of the troops and aircraft in the islands on East Falkland at Port Stanley. This town on the east side of the island held 6,000 men and had the islands' only, if short (4,000 foot), hard surface airfield. There were also significant numbers of troops and aircraft at Goose Green, which had a grass airstrip, and troops on Fanning Head. There was whatever was left on Pebble Island and a reinforced battalion (1,500 men) at

Fox Bay on West Falkland, neither of which saw any part in the coming action.

On the night of 20–21 May there seemingly being no reasonable alternative, the 20 ship British amphibious group—the two assault ships (*Fearless* and *Intrepid*), military and civilian troop and supply vessels (*Canberra, Europic Ferry, Stromness, Elk,* five logistic ships), and escorts—assembled well to the north of the Falkland Sound entrance. The carrier group moved in to their southeast, to give them close support. It was a cold, clear moonlit night, a relief after the storms of the past few days. Under cover of darkness, the amphibious group steamed south, passing Cape Dolphin, one of its escorts bombarding targets ashore at Fanning Head with her 4.5 inch gun as they passed into the Sound.

Several other feints, such as raids by commandos, bombardments by ships and planes, took place at the same time, with the goal of attracting Argentine attention farther south or elsewhere. SBS with artillery observers attached had a sharp battle on Fanning Head just prior to the coming landing, to clear the area. SAS carried out a diversionary operation near Goose Green.

At dawn (0630) on 21 May, led in by the trawler minesweepers, the Royal Navy's Commodore M. C. Clapp (Commodore Amphibious Warfare) finally put a brigade-sized (2,500 men) force of commandos, paratroopers, artillery, Rapier surface-to-air (antiair) missiles, engineers, light tanks, and personnel carriers ashore on three beaches at the small Port San Carlos on East Falkland Island, at San Carlos settlement, and at Ajax Bay. 3 Commando Brigade landed from two assault ships and *Canberra*, Phase I being a simultaneous beach assault by commandos and paratroopers, to seize key terrain overlooking the objective area. In Phase II followup units secured Port San Carlos. Phase III consisted of bringing in artillery and air defense weapons by helicopter. One commando battalion was held in reserve. Surprise was complete. There was little preliminary resistance ashore since the San Carlos area was defended by only a handful of troops, but once the main thrust was identified a full-scale reaction was bound to come.

Once inside the San Carlos roadstead, there was some temporary but unavoidable concentration of ships. These assault ships, troopers, supply vessels, and landing craft were tied to the beachhead and very vulnerable to air attack. However, while the British had little room to maneuver, geography also forced high performance aircraft from the mainland to approach from the west and to attack east up the anchorage axis ("bomb alley" to the British, "death alley" to their foes). This predictability helped somewhat to balance the odds for what everyone knew was coming. It was air attack they most had to fear.

Naval support while the beachhead was being established utilized the standard technique of defense in depth. The outer ring was held by Harriers flying combat air patrol. But without any hope of sufficient fighter cover (although construction of a landing pad was begun ashore at once) Sea Dart, Seawolf, and Sea Cat antiaircraft missile-armed destroyers and frigates had to take up the slack. They did. Once in, the second element was provided by a strong picket—a pair of escorts known as the "missile trap," stationed in the northern entrance to Falkland Sound. This was usually a "22-42 combo," a Type 42 destroyer armed with Sea Dart surface-to-air missiles covered by a Type 22 frigate carrying Seawolf missiles. The picket's job was to give early warning, to help the CAP, and itself to do as much damage as it could. The next ring, the "gunline," comprised three or four ships off the entrance to San Carlos Water, bringing to bear every available missile and gun system. Finally, within the anchorage itself, in "bomb alley," were the assault troop and stores ships' Sea Cats, small caliber guns, and notably the shore-based Rapier fire units. They had not long to wait.

Once day broke enemy pilots had a large and concentrated target; they knew more or less where it had to be, and they could now see it. Beginning at 1000, Argentine pilots flew sortie after sortie against the warships and supply vessels, using everything that would fly. It was a maximum effort, employing types ranging from locally-based Pucaras and Italian-built trainers being now utilized as ground attack planes to Mirage III fighters, A-4 dive bombers and Super Etendard attack craft from the mainland. They used saturation tactics, sortieing as many as 72 aircraft at one time. And, weather permitting, except for an inexplicable day's respite after the landing, they kept it up off and on until the end. Raids on the

25th—Argentine Independence Day—were particularly bad, first *Conventry* then *Atlantic Conveyor* being sunk.

At first the Argentines came in large mixed formations, A-4s in waves of four, high, covered by Mirages. After losing many planes at high altitudes to Sea Darts and Harriers, the big formations were broken up. A-4s and Mirages ended up attacking alone, in pairs, at low level.

Soon ships' superstructures became covered with machine guns of various calibers, acquired from whatever sources. Missile systems forced enemy aircraft to come in low and slow, so that they could really identify their targets and attack accurately. At this point the planes became vulnerable to these machine guns. Even just distracting the pilots was worth the effort.

The Argentine pilots reportedly flew magnificently, coming in over and between the islands, below radar, at times in their attacks seeming to skim right over the British vessels at masthead height. There were few extended dogfights. Argentine pilots, always low on fuel, avoided the Harriers as far as they could, dropped their bombs, and got out. They had little time to acquire their targets. Antiaircraft fire was heavy. Some of their munitions proved to be duds. Yet they hit approximately 75 percent of the surface warships of the task force. Their losses were correspondingly severe, perhaps one-third of their 140 high performance combat jets in all. Although the pilots gave their best effort, it was just not enough.

By the close of the first day at San Carlos, however, the strength and fury of enemy air attacks had stunned the navy. One frigate (*Ardent*) had been sunk, and four damaged. It was decided to withdraw all but two or three of the key immediately unloading supply ships. Working store ships in the anchorage during daylight were from then on to be kept to an absolute minimum. Since 3 Commando Brigade was planning on direct afloat logistic support from ships laying just offshore, this was a blow.

Any experienced military commander knows that the landing force would be at its most vulnerable during its first hours ashore. The gods of war now nodded toward the British. There was at least no evidence whatever of any attempt by Argentine ground forces to mount a counterattack, or to concentrate men by helicopter for a thrust against the beachhead, either then or later. The British were given precious time to reorganize and to rethink their plans.

Therefore, as soon as the necessary troops, equipment, supplies, and ammunition were safely and firmly ashore, the fleet dispersed to sea again, leaving an absolute minimum number of ships for continuing gunfire support, tactical transport, and supply. From then on, for a surface ship—even an armed one—to be caught out alone, in daylight, without air cover, in the Sound or nearby island waters was almost suicide. Those ships that had business there either moved in convoy, kept well out to sea, or stayed close within defended areas such as San Carlos. They did so preferably at night or under conditions of restricted visibility.

Even so, severe losses were still sustained: *Antelope, Coventry,* and *Atlantic Conveyor,* all in the general San Carlos area. At Fitzroy later, two landing ships and a landing craft nearby in Choiseul Bay were discovered by a Westinghouse unjammable surveillance radar, without adequate air cover, or surface support, or shore-based missile defense. In the first Argentine air attack on the fleet in two days, all three were set on fire by bombs and rockets, sunk (*Sir Galahad* and the landing craft) or severely damaged (*Sir Tristram*). Eight other men o'war and another RFA suffered varying degrees of damage, at various locations and times. But these incidents were never quite that critical. Replacement and additional ships arrived steadily.

As soon as practicable, engineers constructed a rudimentary airstrip ashore, on the north shore of San Carlos Water. The strip was 860 feet long, surfaced with aluminum matting, with primitive but adequate refuelling facilities. There were times when the strip held as many as eight or nine Harriers. Helicopters also made use of it.

It was the practice of Harriers launched from the carriers first to take up station either on CAP (Sea Harriers) or airborne orbit (GR3s). After 20 minutes or so, if aircraft were still serviceable and fully armed, they would land on the shore strip to refuel. The next time their fuel ran out, or after any combat, Sea Harriers returned to their carrier. GR3s remained on the strip awaiting a tasking call, thereafter returning to their ship.*

---

*This was a microreplay of Japanese Vice Admiral Jisaburo Ozawa's plan for the Battle of the Philippine Sea (1944), called by us the "Marianas Turkey Shoot."

The original ten mile square beachhead was duly consolidated, built up, expanded; there was a breakout; more army troops (5 Brigade) were landed; and the islands retaken. The battle gradually shifted from an air-sea confrontation to an air-ground one. British troops made a two-pronged, three week drive east across the island, one column north around via Teal Inlet and the other south through Goose Green (where there was a stiff fight). They first captured or drove in outlying units, loosely invested Stanley, then closed in on the garrison (see Appendix I). The cold, wet, boggy ground and the extremely primitive road net made going very slow. The Chinook helicopters that went down with *Atlantic Conveyor* were sorely missed, their loss adding perhaps as much as a week to the whole operation.

At the end the bulk of Argentina's Falkland garrison was driven into a defensive perimeter close around Stanley, their back to the sea. The British advance was supported at every point by heavy and ceaseless pounding from the 4.5 inch guns of bombarding escorts lying close offshore. On 11 June *Glamorgan* was damaged by shore-based Exocet missile, the final naval casualty of the war. Suddenly the Argentines had enough, they broke and ran, everywhere along the line.

A cease-fire was formally requested by the commander of Stanley garrison and granted by the local British commander on 14 June. Argentine forces on the islands were surrendered the following day, considerably demoralized. After just 74 short but crowded days, the affair was all over. The alien flag was hauled down. The Queen's writ had been made to run once again in these cold, barren, distant islands. The lion, well served by his navy, could still roar.

The inner and outer harbors at Stanley soon filled with ships, more then at any time since World War I: *Canberra*, the ferries, frigates, *Intrepid* and *Fearless*, the rusty trawlers now flying the white ensign. Between them and the shore there was the monotonous buzz of commuting small boats, tugs, launches, and landing craft. The continuous clatter of helicopters filled the air.

Even now the work of the fleet was not over. The blockade had perforce to be continued. Mines had to be swept. The 11,400 prisoners had to be disposed of.

Prisoners of war (POWs) were first held on troopers offshore, as well as in camps ashore, hoping that the Argentines would sooner or later officially acknowledge British repossession of the islands. It having soon been decided that the POWs were an unnecessary and profitless burden, various troopers (*Canberra, St. Edmund,* and *Norland*) with the cooperation of the Argentines gradually delivered them home, enlisted men first, then the officers and technicians, and finally senior commanders. They were landed by agreement at the small, isolated mainland town of Puerto Madryn, 650 miles south of Buenos Aires. By 14 July all Argentines were gone.

Just after the middle of June, too, a small temporary mixed task group was detached to evict forcibly the last Argentine toehold in the dependencies—a meteorological station maintained in the South Sandwich chain by the Argentine navy. On 20 June to be exact, British marines were landed on Thule and did the job. Argentina claimed it had obtained permission to establish the weather station in 1977; it was not armed although it did have code gear. There was no resistance. The station was closed. That was that.

Stanley itself suffered relatively little overt physical damage. The airfield, however, was a desolate, windswept place made worse by bombing and shelling. There was now a major task of repair and reconstruction, returning normal service to the fleet and the people. Apart from the shattered water mains, electric power lines and communications had been brought down during the final fighting. Reopening the airport and port were priority items. Repairs and clearning debris were slow affairs, because of mines and booby traps.

All mariners were strongly advised for their own safety to avoid the territorial seas and internal waters around the islands until they were cleared of mines and unexploded ordnance, or until the locations of these dangers to navigation were clearly marked. On this marking and clearing the navy was working, but it was to be a long time before things returned to normal, if ever again they did.

Although no official acknowledgement of the British position by Buenos Aires was forthcoming, on 22 July the blockade was lifted. Argentines were asked anyway to keep 150 miles off the islands without special permission, to avoid misunderstandings and "inadvertent clashes." There was really an armistice, not peace.

In London the Falklands honors list was a long one. Admiral Lewin was made a baron by a grateful sovereign. Admiral Fieldhouse received a GBE. Admiral Woodward and General Moore were knighted. Other decorations (DSOs, CBEs, DSCs, DFCs, and the like) included two Victoria Crosses, both posthumous, both army. Few can have been forgotten, if any, afloat or ashore. Conveyed by these honors was a collective "well done."

OPERATIONAL ASPECTS

In just 74 days the Falklands campaign was all over. In just those short two-and-a-half months we saw the first major naval campaign in nearly 40 years. As a result of that campaign, another most significant corner of naval history has been turned: a surface fleet has stood up to superior hostile air power and won. The strategic importance of this achievement is not always acknowledged. But let us start at the beginning.

A total of 51 ships flying the white ensign and never more than 18 combatants were involved in the Falklands operations. These ships—carriers, escorts, submarines, minesweepers, dispatch vessels, amphibious ships—carried a variety of missiles (Sea Dart, Seawolf, Sea Cat) and 4.5 inch guns. Some carried Ikara, and a surface-to-surface version of Exocet. They carried Harriers and helicopters. Even though largely improvised, it was a remarkably well-balanced fleet, proving flexibility adaptable to a wide variety of tasks. It had to be, steaming in many respects into the unknown as it was. Four were sunk and two seriously damaged early on.

All told, 171 naval aircraft (Sea Harriers and helicopters) were deployed in 14 squadrons. Four of these squadrons were newly organized and had been formed at short notice. Over the whole operation there was 90 percent availability of all embarked aircraft. High states of deck readiness were maintained for long periods. Operational sorties were flown against enemy aircraft, shipping, and shore targets. Flying rates were intensive even in the worst of weather.

For naval professionals, the Royal Navy's everyday operational problems had had special meaning. The decision to set up picket lines and the San Carlos gunline, and the patently necessary compromise therefore assumed to have been made with other tasks; the obvious problems involved in maintaining maximum shipboard readiness conditions for extended periods and again the compromise; the usefulness or otherwise of electronic emission control; and the redemonstrated importance of effective damage control were shared by every caring officer, not only on quiet midwatches and drill duty days.

To sail a fleet great distances at very short notice, to within range of superior hostile air power, there to establish and maintain an opposed blockade and successfully execute one of the largest amphibious assaults since World War II, as the Royal Navy did, is to accept and overcome great risks. Here was no uncertain trumpet.

In the early stages of the conflict, Royal Navy dispositions appeared to be somewhat as follows: (1) 200 or more miles west of the Falklands, between the Falklands and the Argentinian mainland, a picket line of nuclear-powered attack submarines and, closer in, general purpose destroyers, to give the fleet early warning of enemy air attack and to cut off the islands from Argentine surface traffic; (2) the assembling main fleet (carrier battle group, amphibious group) held 100 miles or so to the east of the Falklands, steaming a daily north-south "racetrack" course, out of range of most enemy aircraft based on the mainland, except when the fleet moved in at night to bombard or strafe enemy forces on the islands; (3) providing close escort, blockade patrols, transport, and general gunnery support, the ASW frigates and whatever destroyers could be spared from other duties.

Properly what we saw here was a loose, distant ("open") British military (air and naval) blockade of the Argentine coast, but a total (air, naval, and commercial) close, and continuous blockade of the Falklands. Close blockade is characteristically a method of contesting another's at least local and perhaps temporary command of the sea.

The location and shadowing of the Argentine surface navy was the most vital preoccupation of the British command. If the British blockade (or the preliminary attack on South Georgia) had drawn the Argentine navy out to sea, British submarines stationed outside its bases could have been employed to discourage it from returning to base. This conceivably would have forced the desired conventional primarily naval battle in which the British fleet would have been superior at least in tradition, electronics, and experience, and possibly in numbers.

If the Argentine navy did sortie, one nagging worry was that the enemy carrier would remain in safety 200 miles away—a comfortable range for her A-4s launching air attacks on the fleet. Woodward proposed in this case to withdraw his carriers eastward at speed. Meanwhile, two British "attack groups" would seek to engage the Argentine ships. Originally, one group was to be composed of the three Type 42 destroyers, the second of *Glamorgan* with two Type 21 frigates. Attrition soon drew the sting out of the attack groups.

To gain air superiority against an island enemy, carrier-launched fighter sweeps must strike his airfields, going for planes on the ground and in the air, for ground control (radar) installations, and for AA defenses, paving the way for bombers; bombers then blast the fields, cratering runways and destroying support facilities, paralyzing the fields; standing fighter patrols continue to orbit and strafe, keeping the fields pounded down, "bouncing" anything that tries to use them.

Neither the several runs made on Stanley airfield by the Vulkans nor the repeated attacks by Harriers—using tons of as much as 1,000 pound bombs—ever succeeded in closing Stanley airfield. The enemy had scaped together piles of mud and debris which he bulldozed onto the runway to simulate cratering (there was none), successfully confusing the photo interpreters. The bombs were wrong, too.

Even to accomplish this just at Stanley then, the British lacked the strength. They simply had too few planes. Keeping the carriers at a distance materially lessened the effectiveness of those they did have. Nothing, of course, could be done about Argentine airfields on the mainland. They remained a privileged sanctuary until the end.

Although a few Argentine supply ships (*Bahia Buen Suceso,* as one for instance) apparently did get through the blockade, however, no real continuing large scale Argentine attempt at breaking it was ever made except from the air. Their C-130s did continue to land right up to the last night. Since that appears to have been enough (there seems to have been some maldistribution of supplies but there were no overall shortages), the main impact of the short British blockade must have been psychological, increasing the Falklands garrison's feeling of isolation.

By mid-May, nonetheless, as a strategic deployment to create the expected preconditions for an amphibious landing (gaining and maintaining command of the sea) the British task force must on balance be considered a failure. More than two weeks after their arrival, despite all the minor successes, the constant harassment of the enemy, losses were about even. The bulk of Argentina's sea and air forces remained intact. Stanley airfield was still open. The weather, foul enough, was due to continue to worsen and diplomatic pressure on British could only increase. Argentina had had everything to gain and little to lose by holding back its remaining strength to await the only threat that could not be ignored: a landing. The British decided to go in anyway.

There was later some accidental operational spillover to the blockades. On 8 June the 220,000 DWT U.S.-owned but Liberian-registered supertanker *Hercules,* out of the Virgin Islands bound for Valdez, Alaska in ballast, was 480 miles northeast of the Falklands steaming south. She was attacked there by unknown four engine aircraft. None of the crew was injured but the ship took on a 6° list and headed for Rio de Janeiro, an unexploded 500-lb. bomb in her hull. *Hercules* was far from the mutually declared 200-mile maritime exclusion zones. According to British sources the oil tanker had been sighted and ordered by radio to head for an Argentine port within 15 minutes or face attack. Argentina denied the story. On 2 June, however, an Argentine C-130 had attacked a British tanker within the 200-mile zone under similar circumstances. *Hercules* had eventually to be scuttled at sea.

The landing at San Carlos was in its major outlines much like any other modern assault. The Royal Navy's task was to transport the assaulting troops, their equipment and supplies; protect the passage of the troops and support their landing; and keep communications open for the flow of supplies. The operation was carried out by the traditional four elements: (1) the troops; (2) the amphibious ships and craft (including helicopters); (3) the close escort; and (4) the covering force. Helicopters did play a significant role bringing men and material ashore, but most things came in over the beach as always.

Both assault brigades were landed without loss of a man or one piece of equipment. The really high value targets like *Canberra, Norland, Fearless,* and *Intrepid* were untouched by the enemy. The navy took good care of its wards.

The British air defense problem, always recognized as the critical issue, was compounded by the total absence of what the military normally considered a fundamental requirement; air-superiority fighters like the U.S. F-14 or even the F-18. The force lacked any carrier-borne early warning and fighter direction mini-AWACS aircraft like the Grumman E-2C, or electronic countermeasures planes. Never totaling more than 36 flyable machines, by the landing only some two dozen Harriers could still have been operational at most. Nonetheless, a sufficient defense was managed.

The air battle seldom assumed the formal characteristics of a series of dog fights, with a beginning, middle, and end, and a clear victor. It rather looked like a formless collection of sudden melees, which just as quickly died away. Geography, weapons, and tactics were such that aircraft were never long in sight of each other. Attackers kept out of sight until the last minute and came in low. Defenders pounced on them from above, firing missiles, and left. In such a contest the inherent agility of the Harriers paid off. Between 40 and 50 Argentine aircraft never made it back to base, and half were lost to Harriers.

Even in the electronic age, daylight during clear weather must have been the bad time for the British. Argentinian aircraft lacked any serious night-fighting capability. Except for the handful of French-built Super Etendards, they lacked sufficient radar. It can, therefore, safely be assumed that most British naval activity took place during darkness or other times of low visibility, at least until they gained an airstrip and set up air defenses ashore.

The two British small (light) carriers (*Hermes* and *Invincible*) were effective and flexible command ships, providing at the same time good platforms for air operations. One day, *Hermes* tasked 12 Sea Harriers against shore targets, yet one hour after the aircraft returned, the same planes were airborne for air defense patrols. But the carriers were just too small, and VSTOL-limited. Truly capable AWACS aircraft were beyond them, as has been pointed out.

As a result, surface vessels absorbed the brunt of the first sustained air attacks against a fleet at sea since the end of World War II. In an only imperfectly commanded sea (being very generous), no matter what fleet support the blockade or landing operations might have required, it could never be given to an extent which denied the survival of the covering carrier battle group and its being left free for possible independent action. Remember the hard days at Guadalcanal? Recommendations that the battle group be moved close in and kept there, slugging it out toe to toe with the enemy to the end, were wisely never followed up.

The hardworking destroyers and frigates as usual caught most of the hell. *Sheffield* (4,100 tons) was lost on picket early, as mentioned, and *Coventry* (4,100 tons) during the later San Carlos landing, in actions reminiscent of similar losses of Okinawa in 1945. The 3,200 ton frigates Ardent and *Antelope,* were also sunk, both on the gunline during the war's last phases. They all did close escort, defended the landing force, furnished gunfire support, carried landing parties, and performed the multitude of other tasks normal to these types. Many worked at air defense by day and routine antisubmarine patrolling at night. The story is endless, and the more things change . . .*

There is justifiable concern over the ease with which *Sheffield* and *Coventry* were overwhelmed, for both were modern Type 42 destroyers, intended among other things to help defend not only themselves but also the rest of the fleet against air attack. The case

---

*The hard lying in those small ships was chronicled for all time by Taffrail in his *Endless Story* (London: Hodder and Stoughton, 1938).

of *Sheffield* is tactically most disturbing, for she does not appear to have made the best use of the defensive systems sensors or ECM she had. Another look at the equipment and operating procedures seems in order. *Glamorgan* did better.

Sheffield was sunk by an air-to-surface, sea-skimming anti-ship missile, in a textbook stand off attack, the attackers bobbing up and down just at the radar horizon. The British did not have a radar contact until the fatal missile was already launched, and then it was too late. Damage control proved almost impossible, in any case. *Coventry* was hit by conventional "iron" bombs.

The 4.5 inch guns carried on board most of the destroyers and frigates (all except the three *Broadswords*)—the only large gun available—again proved their worth for shore bombardment, nearly 8,000 rounds being fired. While normally not quite as accurate as shore-based guns, they combine a relatively high rate of fire with a plentiful ammunition supply and they are mobile. In the gunfire support role, no really acceptable substitute has yet been found. Most ships wore out the barrels of their guns.

On the other hand, the single-mount 20mm and 40mm guns the escorts regularly carried were insufficient for last-ditch, close-in antiair point defense, and there were nowhere near enough of them. Manual in operation, they used "iron" sights, and they threw up too low a volume of fire. Those hostile aircraft and missiles which did manage to penetrate the Harrier/missile defense really found nothing else in the last 1,000–1,500 yards to stop them.

Britain's fast, deadly nuclear-powered attack submarines—or at least the threat of them—may have exercised a powerful deterrent effect on Argentine surface navy operations. One or more were indicated as being early on the scene, "about in the waters." The Argentine navy did lose *General Belgrano* to one of them (*Conqueror*). For the rest, the Argentine navy kept well clear of any combat areas. But whether this inactivity was in fact attributable directly in whole or only in part to the submarine threat is difficult to tell. The submarines also patrolled off the coast of mainland Argentina, providing valuable intelligence on likely air attacks to the task force.

Nimrod maritime patrol aircraft were the first to be based on Ascension Island, beginning on 6 April. They were immediately involved as communications links for the deploying nuclear-powered submarines. Thereafter they provided continuous direct support and area surveillance to every major element of the task force to the limit of the aircraft's range. All deployments of small aircraft were given airborne search and rescue cover. Once fitted for airborne refueling, Nimrods provided long range surveillance of the sea areas between the Falklands and the Argentine mainland, especially prior to and during the main amphibious assault. In all, Nimrods mounted a total of 111 sorties in support of the force from Ascension alone.

Helicopters are in constant use in modern combat. In many ways helicopters were irreplaceable. They were deadly, agile gunships. They flew ASW and reconnaissance missions in all weathers. They performed search and rescue. They flew as decoys. Above all they were transports between ships, from ship to shore, and from place to place, ashore. They carried heavy loads up and across difficult terrrain, often under fire. Without helicopters, too, the operation would not have succeeded. There were never enough of them either.*

In this whole operation the ASW effort played the role of silent and unsung labor. Ships and aircraft carried out extensive ASW operations. It was intense, grim, and unceasing, loyally conducted by *Atlantic Causeway,* surface escorts, Nimrod maritime patrol aircraft, and helicopters under the most difficult of circumstances even though with little tangible result. Rough seas quench active sonars, mask passive sonars, and make radar or visual detection virtually impossible. Strong water temperature gradients reflect many false sonar echoes. The threat was real, but no British vessels were ever lost to enemy submarine action. The ability to sustain such operations was proved.

The five stern trawlers taken up from trade for use as minesweepers required very limited conversion to make them suitable for their new task. All five trawlers cooperated as a full

---

*One Sea King helicopter even force landed in southern Chile on 16 May, giving rise to speculation and scenarios that may never be cleared up.

team, towing wire sweeps between them. Numerous fairly deeply laid moored mines were located, cut, and destroyed. Weather conditions considerably hampered operations, but being built for deep sea work in rough weather conditions, the trawlers performed exceedingly well. A good thing, too, because there was nothing else.

The Argentines had taken an interest in unconventional underwater warfare, and the British took appropriate precautions. Outside the Falklands area, ships left anchorages at night and returned during the day, for fear of nocturnal attacks on their hulls. In the combat area, crews threw "scare charges" (grenades) into the water two or three times an hour to deter attack. Divers were sent down to check ships for limpet mines.

The specialized amphibious warfare ships and craft developed in World War II and after, again proved their indispensability in putting troops, equipment, ammunition, and other supplies over a hostile beach. One of the two amphibious assault ships (*Intrepid*), in the process of decommissioning, listed for disposal, was even given a reprieve, reoutfitted and sent south to join her sister (*Fearless*). The navy was very glad it had those two, as well as the six landing ships. While many kinds of vessels can stand in for this role, there is an irreducible minimum number of core naval vessels beneath which one cannot go and still hope to retain a viable amphibious assault capability.

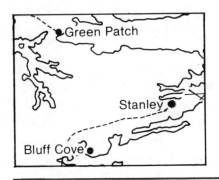

6

Evaluation: Operations & Technology

The Falklands campaign was the first major naval campaign anywhere in nearly 40 years. It provides a critical watershed in naval history. Naval analysts claim many years ago to have anticipated the lessons of the Falklands. We could have predicted the results from our studies, our war games, our maneuvers, and on our simulators. For example, we could have predicted that missiles launched against the British fleet would have a high probability of a hit. But now we have those predictions played out in the real world. There are no technical or tactical surprises, perhaps, but the strategic and tactical results are sometimes very sobering. Some things will never be the same again in our time.

The tragic aspects of this unfortunate piece of history are perhaps clearest in the preliminary politico-military maneuvering, with everyone doing what he thought he had to do to the end. As these roles are played out, it is difficult to see how and where the outcome could have been changed and war avoided.

Preliminary maneuvering in the Falklands first gave the political uses of sea power a good airing. The Argentine navy, who had always had the Antarctic as their exclusive preserve, had already won a toehold on one of the Falklands dependencies. Late in 1976, some 50 meteorologists were put ashore on Thule, in the

South Sandwich group, their presence apparently being regularized the following year. A good presumption seems to be that the Argentine navy originally intended to repeat the Thule tactic only on South Georgia, registering Argentina's claim there as obliquely as possible, confusing and ultimately minimizing British response. With a toehold on each of the dependencies, London would find it the harder to complain about a later naval seizure of the Falklands proper.

Once the situation began to escalate, however, the general deterrent effect of a 90 man detachment of Royal Marines and *Endurance*'s routine presence proved insufficient to prevent the crisis from coming to a head. *Endurance*'s mission to South Georgia then specifically failed to coerce the Argentines into leaving that island. Britain was relying on an expendable trip wire which no one believed was real.

Three and a half decades of politico-military move and countermove had demonstrated the seriousness of the Argentine purpose and their readiness to consider the use of force. The ruling junta's Falklands adventure was almost certainly undertaken in the belief that London would acquiesce in a classic naval *coup de main*, as a *fait accompli*. Britain would not fight for repossession of a colony which, as Buenos Aires saw it, London had been working to divest itself of for years.

One can only speculate as to why the Admiralty did not allow *Endurance*'s helicopters to attack *Guerrico* or *Bahia Paraiso* during the confrontation off South Georgia. Missiles fired from more than one helicopter (*Endurance* carried two helos) on different bearings will certainly confuse even a small combatant's defenses. If successful, this could have at least temporarily run the Argentines off, altering the immediate balance in British favor, and earlier, perhaps before things had got out of hand.

It would then have been so simple and neither the first nor last time that a surprised government had disavowed the suddenly embarrassing and "certainly unauthorized" acts of a distant commander, withdrawn its forces, and forwarded its deepest regrets. London would have been only too happy to accept the apology at its face value.

Two much more fundamental factors determined the outcome of this maneuvering: the overall regional balance of military strength was clearly in Argentina's favor, as was the balance of perceived interests on either side. Those in the Casa Rosada saw little to fear from far-off Britain, and they wanted those islands. In the end, all the sometimes frantic politico-military signally came to naught.

Would the outcome of *Operacion Rosario* have been significantly different if Buenos Aires, instead of its display of overwhelming military strength, had sent to the Falklands just a minimum politico-military symbol of its determination to have the islands, employing only enough force to quietly disarm the few British marines, installed a benevolent civil administration with a minimum police unit, and then withdrawn its troops at once? As was later suggested by a leading Briton, it became almost obligatory for London to respond to such a flagrant military challenge with force. Would it perhaps not have been politically much more difficult so to react to a less military Argentine tactic? Who can really say?

In the end, the ultimate readiness actually to resort to large scale force that must underly all naval suasion—ready or not—the British felt they had to break out.* From politico-military signalling, emphasis shifted to the military uses of sea power, to the ultimate compellence: ejection or destruction of Argentine forces. This transition was actually marked by the deliberate "political" pace of the British mobilization, and particularly that of the scratch lead echelon of the fleet into the crisis area, giving naval suasion its last futile chance to head off a war.

Up until 1940 this actual movement of the British fleet south ready for war would probably have been enough to quietly force settlement of the issue in London's favor. A modern, balanced, sufficient surface fleet would then indeed operate anywhere, do anything, as long as there was water under the great ships' keels. Then during the course of just two years, that all completely changed.

---

*The term is Edward N. Luttwak's, developed in his *The Political Uses of Seapower* (Baltimore: Johns Hopkins University Press, 1974).

In 1940 the British hurriedly assembled an expeditionary force much like the Falklands force and sent it off to Norway with the full might of the fleet in support. By the time the fleet was deployed, the Germans had captured Norwegian air bases, and for the first time in history the fleet was in range of land-based enemy bombers and beyond the range of fighter escort. Lacking adequate air support, the force was badly mauled and withdrew after two months.

Before the Norwegian campaign was over, although few major warships were actually sunk directly by bombs alone, the Germans succeeded in sinking an aircraft carrier, two cruisers, one sloop, and nine destroyers through a variety of means. They damaged six cruisers, two sloops and eight destroyers, the majority through air attack. Such losses could not be regularly borne.

The Norwegian campaign, followed by the air siege of Malta the Greek campaign, the operations of Crete, and then the surprise attack on Pearl Harbor, and the destruction of *Prince of Wales* and *Repulse,* showed in and rammed home a new order of sea power. No surface fleet could any longer operate—especially conduct an opposed amphibious assault—without a least temporary and local air superiority of its own. No guns could defend a fleet alone. No fleet could operate without either adequate organic aircraft or shore-based air cover.

To turn this around, there was now a new operational rule growing out of one overriding fact: as long as a sophisticated military power held command of the air above the sea, no hostile surface fleet could any longer effectively perform its traditional role.

Shore-based air power was almost *ipso facto* superior. To this aircraft carriers provided part of the answer. But since shore-based air usually operated on interior lines, and since the physical requirements of carrier operations inevitably make shipborne aircraft type for type somewhat less than the equal in performance of shore-based air, it ordinarily took a considerable quantitative carrier-borne superiority to defend a fleet against shore-based air.

Until the early 1960s these new operational limitations did not apply to carrier force projection operations off the Third World. There the very apparent gross imbalance in military power—the sophisticated carriers of the larger Western powers, and their numerous air wings—gave both qualitative and quantitative superiority automatically. Although shore-based, the small crude air forces of smaller states simply could not conduct any kind of sustained opposition: the capabilities of both individual carrier aircraft and the carriers as a unit were patently too great for them to face.

Then between the early 1960s and the early 1980s, in the space of perhaps 20 years, for a combination of reasons it is not necessary to go into, the average numerical size of small power air forces increased considerably. In addition, the previous clear technical superiority of naval aircraft belonging to the larger powers was eroded by the widespread introduction of relatively advanced first-line planes into the smaller air forces. The military balance seemed to have shifted, here, too.

From the early 1960s to the early 1980s, even when due allowances were still made for the often only few and small remaining qualitative differences in such things as crew skills, electronics, and fighter direction, it was generally accepted that even in Third World force projection situations, naval air power had lost its net quantitative and qualitative edge. The same rule, it seemed, now applied everywhere: no surface fleet could any longer operate anywhere against superior sophisticated air power.* The Falklands completely reversed that idea.

The British in the Falklands, 40 years after Crete, could in no way be said to have had numerical superiority. They had absolutely no high performance fighters, and they almost certainly never had more than three dozen VSTOL Harriers operational at the same time. The Harriers had never before been tested in combat. And they had their surface-to-air missiles.

The Royal Navy never did gain clear command of Falklands waters. Rather, it suffered its more or less inevitable losses stoically, landed, and supported a landing force. If those troops had not so quickly defeated the Argentine garrison, or if there had even been another long Anzio-type stalemate, the outcome might not have been nearly the same. We shall come back to this later.

---

*Luttwak, pp. 49–51.

But as was very clearly demonstrated in the Falklands, *where a sufficient modern, VSTOL and missile-armed surface fleet is able and willing to take the losses, it can once again operate within a hostile air enviroment,* outstay attacking first-line aircraft, and do what it has to do, anywhere. Evidently this would include the Soviets' VSTOL carrier fleet, too. There is once again a new order of sea power for those willing and able to exploit it.

Before we leave this conceptual area, however, it should be carefully noted that there has been nothing whatever to show that where an opponent has a full working command of the sea (even just local and temporary) the hazard of such enterprises is any less. In the Falklands, until their hold was broken by naval and air action, or allowed by the Argentines to go by default, major British operations (blockade and amphibious assault) could not rationally have been undertaken.

In all this Falklands fighting, neither side ever formally declared war. Wars are seldom any longer acknowledged, but large scale hostilities conducted at a high level of intensity for a significant period of time is war, whatever name it is given. This particular war was kept limited in every way. Geographically the war was almost exclusively confined to the Falklands area. No major operations took place on or over the mainland. Militarily, no nuclear weapons were employed; conventional arms proved sufficient for the job. Politically, neither homeland was ever threatened, nor were the independence, way of life, or other essential interests of either side, except for the islands themselves. The limits were clear. This was a classic example of a "small war."

The U.S. Navy was re-taught some bitter lessons during our landing at Lingayan Gulf (Luzon, January, '45), the first of which was that the best method for suppressing enemy shore-based air in such an operation was on the ground, neutralizing their bases beforehand so that serious strikes cannot be mounted from them against us. Otherwise, as they did in the Gulf, they will wait until we are fully committed to a landing before they hit us, catching us tied to the beaches, when they cannot easily be dealt with, and their targets are many. The British knew this, too. Not to take out those nearby Argentine mainland bases here was courting disaster. But the political—never mind military— costs of doing so were then considered to be too high.

In successful limited war, geographic conditions must allow the attacker to restrict the amount of force with which he has to deal. Islands perfectly meet these conditions; they are easily isolated by a strong navy, leaving only the defending garrison already in place to be faced. This was exactly what was tried in the Falklands, twice, once by either side.

Simply blockading the Falklands, however, would soon have imposed an unacceptable strain on the British task force. For the fuel alone, one tanker/oiler per combatant per month would have been needed. Operations in one of the world's worst sea areas in winter weather would have taken their toll, and it would have taken considerable time for a blockade to have any significant effect.

In a prolonged South Atlantic campaign, a full scale British advanced base could and would have to have been constructed on South Georgia to include an airfield capable of handling high performance fighters, bombers, patrol aircraft, and transports, as well as VSTOL and rotary wing aircraft. A project of considerable technical difficulty, construction of an airfield would have demanded a major commitment of manpower and equipment. It would have taken more time than the British felt they had, indefinitely prolonged the war, and thereby significantly altered the nature of their effort. They did without the field.

That left the Royal Navy with the most common situation in naval warfare: not a commanded sea, but an uncommanded one, with sea control in running dispute. With a reasonable naval force, the ability to carry out blockade and landing operations over an uncommanded sea evidently remains. In a maximum effort, the navy could exercise a limited control of the surface of the sea around the Falklands, even if it did not control the skies above, or the depths.

The direct storming of East Falkland Island—the Argentine stronghold—without adequate air cover could have resulted in very heavy casualties on both sides. Yet the growing danger of attrition by weather and enemy action putting a sustained blockade beyond thought, it seemed increasingly likely that the island would have to be taken by amphibious assault—by the bayonet. The British must have considered landing troops at night on one of the more remote Falklands, or even on West Falkland, quietly building an airstrip for their Harriers, as in the Second World War, and only then going on to take East Falkland. In the end, they elected not to. Such a strategy would take too much time, and would have risked an eventual stand off.

The British chose the San Carlos area on the northwest side of East Falkland for their landing in part, no doubt, because it was the lesser of several evils. He who held Stanley controlled the islands. It lay on the most important of the islands and it offered the quickest, most practicable solution to the strategic problem. But a direct assault on Stanley was out, the British lacked the strength, and too many islanders would get hurt. San Carlos had been looked at years earlier, and was noted then as having what passed in the Falklands as fairly good land routes to Stanley, unfortunately still some 50 miles to the east, where the bulk of the Argentine army was dug in. But also there was a small port, good beaches, and the approach—San Carlos Water—offered a very necessary, sheltered, easily defended, extensive deepwater anchorage. They seem to have chosen well. It was all over only 24 days later.

The Falklands experience gave added impetus to an idea long overdue for general acceptance: regularly using shore-based aircraft of all types in addition to maritime patrol aircraft to directly as well as indirectly support naval combatants in the struggle for command of the sea. Argentine Super Etendards armed with "smart" missiles to sink individual naval vessels, as well as the Canberras, A-4s, and others armed with conventional "iron" bombs, cannon, and rockets, were all shore-based. All of the British RAF planes were shore-based, except the GR3s.

The overwhelming need here is to bridge the historically deep conceptual gap between air force (especially strategic air) and navy roles in the war at sea. In the West up to now air force contributions have too often been indirect, as the air people fought their own war. Help has been limited to large scale bombing of navy-related factories, shipyards, bases, and ports, and to mining ports, traffic approaches, and other shipping choke points. As the Soviets have known for years, this can no longer be enough.

In World War II, the use of heavy bombers left a lot to be desired. Why were the German submarine pens in France and Norway not bombed during construction, when they were vulnerable, rather than later when it was too late? Why was the mid-Atlantic convoy air cover gap allowed to continue long after the heavy bombers to close it were available? Evidently, air force priorities were elsewhere.

In World War II shore-based, non-navy-subordinated tactical fighters and light bombers did frequently attack and sink both individual naval vessels and merchant ships, once in the Bismarck Sea even turning back a large South Pacific convoy. But after the war this use of shore-based aircraft seems largely to have disappeared from active operational plans. Why do we not regularly employ air force heavy bombers for over-water long-range reconnaissance and surveillance? Why are we just now arming them with "smart" missiles for antiship missions long distances at sea? The Soviets manage it. They even employ shore-based fighters in naval roles. Why cannot we?

Objectively, if shore-based, shore-oriented air is available, it is potentially too powerful a weapon to be carelessly left out of the sea fight. More can obviously be done, at the heavy bomber as well as the fighter level. How can we not integrate our available heretofore independent and generally under used shore-based air power into sea power?

But again there must be a caveat. The Falklands also demonstrated the present relative ineffectiveness of shore-based air operating at sea long distances from its shore bases. Postive control of tactical air was not ever attained. Given the large number of Argentine fighter/attack aircraft against the small number of British Harriers (a ratio of at least four to one) and the British lack of AWACS, missiles or no, Argentine results were poor. Even then most of the ships sunk seem to have been lost to a handful of navy pilots. Bravery is not enough.

Argentine air command and control seems to have been too divided, too rigid, and too slow in reacting to opportunities as they opened up. Why did the navy fail to provide the air force with the radar direction that its pilots expected? Why was a whole day's grace allowed the British the day following the San Carlos landing? Why did the navy mount its Super Etendard and other strikes without coordinating with the air force? Why were the landing ships at Fitzroy not attacked earlier (they sat there most of a day)?

Command, control, and communications techniques, tactics, and training will all have to improve markedly before most shore-based air can hope to be anywhere nearly as effective in this role as trained, experienced, sea-oriented air, equalling naval maritime patrol or organic carrier-borne air. Otherwise, this idea will not work. Shore-based air support of naval operations is difficult at best.

One major operational issue was not really settled in the far, cold South Atlantic: the proper role of submarines in conventional naval war. The British counted on them for deterrence. London indicated use of fast nuclear-powered attack submarines reportedly somewhere "about in the area" to enforce their blockade in the interim between its anouncement and the arrival of their surface fleet. This cannot have been one of their most successful moves, and no ships were in fact sunk by submarines then.

Submarines indeed have the potential to be extremely deadly weapons of war. They are quintessential war fighting tools. They can very efficiently sink ships. They are not well-suited to lesser measures, to first stopping suspicious or even known enemy merchant ships, visiting and searching, and if warranted taking those ships prize. Neither are they suited to giving warning and fully providing for the safety of passengers (if any) and crew before sinking those ships, as civilized law requires. Operating submerged, they are invisible, and even poor instruments for establishing a naval presence.

Another factor whose importance here should not be minimized is the considerable odium that attaches to any submarine warfare, especially against merchantmen. This raises considerably the political threshold at which submarines are acceptable. The British, in two long and stressful world wars, went to great lengths to cultivate such a policy, and with it they, and we, must now live.

In the still low-intensity politico-military situation existing up to 1 November, submarines were just out of place. To sink ships without warning—the only way submarines can effectively operate, or even establish a presence—would have been to fight a war at a level that the remainder of the international political apparatus had not yet reached. The British could not afford this.

Then on 2 May, with time running out, *General Belgrano* was sunk, by *Conqueror,* well outside the 200-mile exclusion zone, "Copenhagened" in the tradition of Nelson and Fisher. Had it not been for what immediately followed, Britain's strong diplomatic position and support from its allies would have been seriously hurt. Argentina swiftly replied, deliberately sinking *Sheffield* on 4 May, nicely taking London off the hook.

The Argentines had to be fully aware that within a couple of weeks of their seizure of the islands at least one or two British nuclear-powered attack submarines would be keeping close watch on their naval bases. This knowledge did not inhibit them from sailing their fleet. Only after *General Belgrano* was sunk could it be said that the submarines contributed any deterrence. Submarines are little or no deterrent in anything less than a hot war.

Conqueror's sinking of *Belgrano* and the Argentine response did effectively signal a shift into a more serious phase of hostilities, but up to that point, London's announcement regarding its use of submarines did cause a certain amount of nervous restlessness among its friends. After that, anything went.

The last and overriding comment must, therefore, be that the traditional value of sea power has in recent years in no way diminished. Sea power's form has continued to adjust to new weapons and tactics, but command of the sea—the ability to use the sea as one likes and to deny this to an enemy—however gained and exercised, is in water areas, still the most important factor. How else could Britain's power have been projected successfully over an extended period, against a worthy enemy, 8,000 miles from the home base?

TECHNOLOGY

Every modern war occurs in a period of transition from what has been to what will be. Any war is, therefore, a data point in a stream of scientific and technical change beginning long before and continuing long afterwards. This stream now moves at an ever faster rate. The Falklands affair is no exception, occuring in an especially early and therefore crude stage of development of VSTOL and missile warfare. It is all the more fascinating for that, giving us an opportunity to look far ahead and found our view on an unusually rich data base.

At the technical level, this was clearly a high technology, high cost war, a fact announced by all the media. Surface vessels defended themselves against the most modern aircraft and submarines. Aircraft were high performance conventional as well as VSTOL and helicopter, armed with air-to-air and air-to-surface missiles and rockets, as well as bombs and guns. Submarines were nuclear-powered, carrying wireguided as well as conventional torpedoes. As mentioned, ships relied extensively on surface-to-air missiles for area, point, and close-in defense. Computer array faced computer array.

Yet the importance of the existing broad technical base underlying all modern fleet operations remained the same. The mass of better known, somewhat more standard machinery and equipment (many were not long out of the technical innovation class) also played its expected role: all the new electronics (radar, radio navigation, communications) gear, and gas turbine propulsion, just to name two. Navigators, communicators, pilots, and engineers on both sides all obviously drew on a modern and quite familiar professional base, the technical content of which was in no way diminished. Only technically advanced powers could have fought this war this way, building on what came before.

The Falklands conflict was the first involving large numbers of fighting ships powered by gas turbines. Fifteen of the Royal Navy's major combatants were so powered, including *Invincible.* No engines had to be changed during the actual period of hostilities. The value of gas turbines in getting a ship out of trouble or pressing home an attack—from idle to full speed took only 90 seconds—was here amply proven.

The navy successfully utilized an Inmarsat communications satellite, on which it leased capacity, for its ultra-high frequency communications to the fleet. Both naval and merchant ships carried transmitter/receiver terminals capable of handling voice, telex, facsimile, and data. Most traffic was telex. Although difficult to intercept, there was some interference with the radars. For the navy to have laid hands on all those additional terminals at such short notice must be considered something of a coup.

Most things remained the same, of course. One of the representative, more prosaic examples not materially altered was coastal navigation and piloting. Eight new charts of the Falklands area had been published within the previous five years, and two others had new editions, one as late as 2 April. The available charts were evidently adequate to support the fleet without any reported serious losses of ships or men through missing or inaccurate data or uncharted dangers. The mariners could not have done without such a broad technical base, established over the years.

There were the usual technical problems on both sides. Unexploded bombs were found in the hulls of at least six British vessels. Argentine bombs were generally 13 years old, and were designed for use against land targets. They sometimes did not have enough time in flight to properly arm. Some had delay fuzes. Some were fuzed to explode only after absorbing more impact than that offered by the thin sides of modern British ships. Some went right through and out the other side. On the other hand, the soft boggy terrain of East Falkland is littered with unexploded British bombs and shells. AS-12 missiles went right through *Santa Fe*. There are reports that even British torpedoes had problems.

In innovation, aircraft and their missiles led the way on both sides. Aircraft carried heat-seeking and radar-homing missiles for use against ground targets, ships, or other planes. In defense they could fire magnesium flares to confuse heat-seeking missiles, or they could jam radar. Some missiles were fuzed so they could detonate without actually striking their target, turning a near miss into a hit; that is, they had proximity as well as impact fuzes.

Of all the naval weapon systems employed by the British in the Falkland Islands affair, the shortlegged, sub (or trans) sonic VSTOL Harrier must be judged the most outstanding. Without it, the British would certainly have lost the war. An eventual total of 28 Sea Harriers and 14 RAF Harrier GR3s were deployed to the battle area. Harriers, of course, flew surface reconnaissance and attack missions, their originally intended role. In addition, carrying U.S.-built Sidewinder air-to-air missiles and two 30 mm cannon, they effectively provided an ad hoc combat air patrol, even against Mirage IIIs.

The Sea Harrier is classified as a single wing attack aircraft, with a wingspan of 25 feet, a length of 46 feet, and a height of 11 feet, weighting 23,100 pounds, capable of flying out at mach 0.96 (mach 1.2 diving). It has a practical maximum ceiling of 50,000 feet. Its range taking off vertically is 50 to 100 miles; with a short take-off run, it is 250 miles. There is a severe range/load trade-off, but the Harrier can carry as much as 5,000 pounds of ordnance.

For the statistically minded, Harriers flew over 2,000 sorties under extremely demanding weather conditions, in hastily improvised attack and defense profiles, from carriers and forward staging ships operating in sea states and under steaming conditions that might have halted normal carrier operations. They flew an average of 55 hours per aircraft per month and six sorties per day. They achieved 80 percent availability 8,000 miles from their principal maintenance base.

In the Falklands neither side really had local control of the air. Always inferior in numbers, the Harriers did not keep Argentine aircraft totally off either the ships or the beaches. The Harriers did continually disrupt the attackers' approach runs, and they did exact a serious toll for Argentine successes. They bombed and strafed on their own, making runs on Argentine airfields and elsewhere in the Falklands. They allowed the air defense issue to be settled by other means, mainly, missiles.

The Harrier's maneuverability, advanced avionics, and U.S. Sidewinders made them more than a match for the aircraft launched against them. Harriers destroyed perhaps one-half (20–30) of all the enemy actually shot down. While five were lost to ground fire and four were noncombat losses, none of the Harriers were lost to enemy planes. Although severe limitations in the range/load trade-off remain, VSTOL strike aircraft are here to stay.

Ski-jump ramps fitted to the carriers contributed materially to Harrier operations at sea. Launch over these ramps greatly reduced take-off failure. Cockpit workload and difficulties of timing in leaving a flat deck at the correct moment in the pitching cycle would otherwise have been considerably greater. So would the risk.

While British vessels were certainly lost from bomb and rocket, it was the Argentinian French-built air-to-surface version of the over-the-horizon seaskimming Exocet cruise missile that proved to be the most dangerous single naval weapon. The Exocet AM 39 missile is a "fire and forget" 15.5 foot, 1,440 pound pilotless aircraft. It can be launched from a plane flying anywhere between 33,000 and 300 feet. It has a maximum range of 30 to 44 miles, depending on the altitude and speed of the launching aircraft.

To launch, the parent aircraft simply programs the Exocet with target range and bearing. The missile is released and the pilot departs for base. The missile drops to about five to six feet above the sea, flying at just below the speed of sound. Eight miles from target, the missile's own radar system takes over for terminal guidance. It is difficult to detect and almost impossible to stop.

The Argentine navy had actually ordered 40 Exocets from the French as early as 1980. Ten had arrived before the Falklands conflict, and ten more were about to be sent. It had also ordered a total of 14 delivery systems—Super Etendard naval strike aircraft—of which only six had been delivered before the EEC embargo took effect. Five more had been due at the end of May.

Although of five air-to-surface Exocets fired, only three struck their intended targets, a fourth struck a ship it was not aimed at (a hulk?), and one missed entirely (decoyed?), *Sheffield* and *Atlantic Conveyor* were both lost to Exocets. The Exocets that sank *Sheffield* and *Conveyor* were fired by Etendards from distances of about 20 to 26 miles. In both cases, a single strike was sufficient for the job.

Sheffield's story has been released at length, and it seems worth setting out in some detail here. Two Super Etendards picked up *Sheffield* on their radar and locked on. Both pilots fired at radar blips rather than at the ship, and then disappeared without observing the results. Warning was short, although only one missile completed its run.

For one thing, *Sheffield*'s main air-search radar was temporarily turned off to allow the Inmarsat satellite communications link to be used. *Hermes* was providing her with a radar picture by means of data-link but the ship did not have a solid, recognizable contact until the fatal missile was already launched. Then despite the fact that the incoming missile had already been detected on ESM equipment, nothing appears to have been done to alert the defense until too late. ("Too late" is often heard in relation to missile defence.) The ship's crew had only time to take cover.

Four or five seconds later the thin-skinned missile hit, traveling at nearly the speed of sound, tearing a hole fifteen by four feet in the ship's side. Although its warhead apparently failed to detonate, several explosions were touched off anyway by the missile's unspent burning fuel. Directly damaged were two large compartments amidships, including the damage control center, and the ship's main fuel tanks. All the lights went out.

Within seconds, the center of the ship was filled with blinding, choking smoke and fumes from the ship's own fuel, cable insulation, furniture, deep fry fat, and other items. The deck became unbearably hot. Parts of the hull became white hot. Rapidly spreading fires threatened the ammunition lockers. Pressure on the fire main was quickly lost. All power was lost. The crew had steadily to give ground in their battle to save the ship, even though a frigate came alongside to help fight the fire.

Five hours later the captain gave the order to abandon. Of the ship's complement of 270 officers and men, as many as 20 died and 24 were wounded. *Sheffield* did not sink by herself; the hulk had to be finished off later with scuttling charges.

One result of this was that Argentina began early to scour the world arms markets for replacements as its small missile stock quickly ran down. The price of an Exocet on the black market ran to several times list, based on $200,000 each. Some shipments (from Europe) were stopped en route, some (from Latin America) perhaps not.

Not all air-to-surface missiles were carried on fixed-wing platforms. British helicopters (Lynxes) reportedly fired a total of seven light seaskimming antiship Sea Skua missiles at smaller targets. Each one scored a hit, sinking one vessel and damaging the rest. In Royal Navy service for less than a year, they operated well under appalling weather conditions, including a strike by night, in a storm, and with a high sea state. Gazelle helos successfully employed the lighter AS-12 missile.

Then there were the surface-launched missiles. Warships on both sides carried modern computerized central integrated combined weapons management systems linked to radar, sonar, and other sensors, capable of identifying targets in all three dimensions and allocating the most appropriate available weapons to the hostile ones. Their self-homing heat-seeking, sonar, acoustic or radar-directed missiles could sink a hostile ship or submarine or down a threatening aircraft as soon as either they or it came over the horizon. In the Falklands, of course, only the British antiair system really received a workout.

While it is characteristic of antiship cruise missile attacks that the missiles do not arrive in large numbers, they do come in very low on the water and at very high speed. The launching plat-form—above, on, or below water—is able to recognize when its missile is picked up by a target's antiair search radar, signalling the initiation of countermeasures, but a hostile platform, especially a submarine, survives in part by avoiding being picked up itself. It therefore, quite understandably, resists making any elec-tromagnetic emissions not mandatory and exercises strict control of any that are made. It is often reluctant to jam, so as not to give away its position. In order to defeat such attacks, the antiair missile system can be simple but must above all react at once. It must be fast.

For air defence in general, missiles were more effective in the Falklands than guns. That much is now clearly proven. Warships were themselves really defended not by the 4.5 inch or machine guns but by high speed, computer-fired missile systems that responded "instantly" to a radar target, selecting the most threatening one(s), assigning the most effective counter, and sometimes even automatically taking the required action. None of the systems, of course, were tested against other missiles.

British troops were equipped with land-based radar-directed antiair missiles systems of their own and even carried shoulder-fired antiair missiles. The Argentines had coast defense versions of the Exocet missile, one of which hit and damaged *Glamorgan* in the final phases of the battle. At times it must have seemed that there were missiles everywhere, being employed for every offensive and defensive purpose. One presumes that even Ikara (an ASW missile) got a workout at some point, during the *San Luis* case, perhaps.

The most important British antiair missile was the heavy, long range Sea Dart, carried by the larger ships. According to seemingly valid claims, Sea Dart missiles destroyed at least eight Argentine aircraft. Sea Dart denied the enemy the advantages of high level reconnaissance and high level air attack. It imposed upon enemy aircraft penalties to fuel consumption and tactical choice. It forced them to use patterns of approach and strike that significantly in-creased their vulnerability to the low level, close range systems and enabled these systems to account for larger numbers of aircraft than otherwise.

Short range, low altitude, lighter Seawolf missiles were next in importance. They can overtake and destroy an artillery shell in flight. Although only mounted on the *Broadswords* and *Andromeda,* they had five or more kills, proving outstandingly effective against aircraft attacking at high speeds and low level seaskimming heights, virtually without radar warning. Their speed of response and deadly accuracy at very close ranges were evident in the fact that, despite many determined attacks, the three Seawolf-armed ships suffered only minor damage from the air.

In the Falklands, seaborne area defense was based on longer range missiles (limited in range to the radar horizon) and was, therefore, provided the British by Sea Dart. Although already good, it could have been better; its computer is rumored to have proven a little slow under combat conditions. Sea Dart reloaded rapidly enough, but its guidance radar could not shift to a new target until the first one had been destroyed and therefore disappeared from the screen. With several planes attacking simultaneously, one was bound to get through. Sea Dart could not hit anything flying at under 2,000 feet.

Closer-in-point defense followed, mainly with Seawolf. Seawolf, however, seemed capable of only defending the ship on which it was mounted. Its guidance computer could be saturated if targets attacked from several directions at once.

Sea Cat, Seawolf's more numerous predecessor, already obsolescent, proved much too slow. Essentially dependent on manual guidance, with a maximum range of perhaps three miles, it was nowhere near Seawolf's equal. Although numerous, it made only perhaps six kills.

Land-based Rapier missiles, which had already seen action in the Persian Gulf area, scored at least another nine kills. An ultra-low-level battlefield defense weapon system, it was landed with the first assault troops. Even after eight weeks at sea as deck cargo in steadily worsening weather, it demonstrated excellent mobility, speed into action, simplicity of operation, robustness, and ease of service which were of decisive importance to British success.

Like the Harriers, most of the missile systems were being used in combat for the first time. Exaggerated battle claims are not unknown, but it is clear that like the Harriers the missiles were good, contributing in a major way to the outcome and easily justifying their proponent's seemingly outrageous claims. This war was high tech, and high cost. Some things will never be the same again.

Finally, in the Falklands modern naval vessels were found to be very complex "one hit" ships. They *are* crowded with wiring, cables, and electronics, making them extremely vulnerable and difficult to keep operating once hit. Damage control had a very good work out. While many of the British standards and practices were shown to be correct, some were not. Wars are won by those who make the fewest mistakes, even here.

A number of serious questions were raised concerning several aspects of British combatant ship construction, damage control, and firefighting techniques. Ships tended to be cramped and, on balance, still too fragile, with too little redundancy of systems. Older ships withstood battle damage better than newer ones. This cannot have escaped the Admiralty's notice.

The unavoidable fragility of modern ships and the power of modern weapons is not an excuse for poor damage control, but a reason for increased attention in this area. Here, too, the Admiralty will certainly agree.

Most escorts now carry the helicopters necessary for ASW, capable of carrying dunking sonar and dropping weapons. From now on, the hum and whir of missile launchers seeking targets, the locking on, the slam and whoosh as missiles are launched in clouds of smoke and flame, the quiet flight of missiles after their targets, the ball of fire as missiles hit, the reload and new target search will mark naval warfare's future. The total removal of large caliber (such as 4.5 inch) guns from the future surface construction should be resisted, however. And a close-in weaponry system (CIWS) should be added to all intended for harm's way.

This idealized requirement does build on current British destroyer and frigate ship construction trends, the invaluable destroyers tending to be multipurpose and therefore larger, the more numerous frigates specialized and smaller. In the end, there are just never enough of either of them.

PHOTOGRAPHS

1. HMS *Hermes* in the South Atlantic. Note ski-jump ramp forward and landing craft aft, as well as Harriers on deck. *Fort*-class fleet replenishment ship in background.

Ministry of Defence (London) photograph

2. HMS *Invincible* leaving for Falklands. Note her ski-jump ramp forward and aircraft (Harriers and Sea Kings) on deck. Sea Dart launcher on forecastle.

Courtesy Dr. R. L. Scheina

3. ARA *25 de Mayo* pierside earlier, at an Argentine base. Note her distinctively tall mast and funnel.

4. HMS *Intrepid* at anchor earlier in a Norwegian fjord, with her four (4) LCUs alongside.

Ministry of Defence (London) photograph

Ministry of Defence (London) photograph

5.   A Type 42 destroyer (HMS *Cardiff*), with 4.5 inch gun and Sea Dart forward.

Ministry of Defence (London) photograph

6. (above) HMS *Broadsword* (Type 22 frigate) coming home. Note Exocet and Seawolf launchers forward and total absence of large caliber gun.

7. (below) A Type 21 frigate (HMS *Arrow*), with Exocet and 4.5 inch gun forward, Sea Cat aft.

Ministry of Defence (London) photograph

Ministry of Defence (London) photograph

8. A Naval Air Arm Sea Harrier (FRS1) in flight. Note different nose from GR3.

Ministry of Defence (London) photograph

9. An RAF Harrier GR3, operating from *Hermes*. Sea Harriers were developed from the RAF version.

10. (above, left)
A French Navy
Super Etendard,
armed with Ex-
ocet, ready for
catapulting. *25
de Mayo* could
not yet handle
Etendards.

11. (above, right) An Exocet AM 39 under the wing of a
Super Etendard. Note Etendard's folding wing.

12. (above) A U.S. Navy A-4 Skyhawk. Argentine naval A-4Qs were similar. Note air-to-air refuelling probe, also present on Argentine model.

14. RMS *Canberra* taking on fuel at sea from RFA *Tidespring*. Note *Canberra*'s two helicopter pads.

Ministry of Defence (London) photograph

13. HMS *Endurance* in ice, date unknown, with her helicopter hangar doors partially open. She carried two helos.

Ministry of Defence (London) photograph

15.   Converted container ship *Atlantic Conveyor* moving out of Devonport headed for the Falklands. Note VSTOL pad forward.

16. Requisitioned ferry *Norland* sailing from Portsmouth with men of 2nd Parachute Battalion.

Ministry of Defence (London) photograph

17.   (left) RFA *Pearleaf* leaving for the Falklands. Note refuelling at sea (ras-ing) gear.

18.   (below) School cruise ship *cum* hospital ship *Uganda* in her Falklands livery. She was converted at Gibraltar.

19. Vulcan/Phalanx, an all-weather, bolt-on, automatic CIWS, firing. Note radar dome.

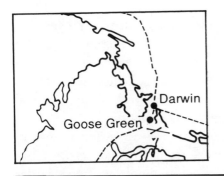

7

Logistics

Early on, "Fleet" established a logistics support "cell," at Northwood. This was an ad hoc triservice organization headed by a Force Logistic Coordinator. Its task was to oversee replenishment planning and all logistic requirements for the task force. Having such a logistics "czar" ensured optimum and economical use of sometimes scarce resources and the priority for supply of the most urgent stores. Over the whole of the campaign at the force level, anyway, no weapon system ran out of ammunition, no ship out of fuel; equipment and spares were maintained at high levels. But what arrangements were made from there down?

Some logistics aspects of the Falklands operation we, the general unofficial naval public may never know, as media coverage had concentrated on more exciting and therefore more newsworthy questions. What, specifically, for instance, were the inescapable logistic problems? The difficulties of maintaining a supply line over 8,000 miles—an average of 21 days sailing time—must have been immense. Some of the logistic arrangements we do know. Larger than anticipated stocks of material were in fact needed. Rates of usage, particularly of conventional ammunition, missiles, and ASW weapons, were markedly higher than expected. Helicopters were sometimes desperately few.

Was the equipment wastage rate as great as in the 1973 Arab–Israeli War? Does the rate substantiate a trend? Did British missile resupply systems hold up? In light of the British experience, are U.S. contingency planning figures realistic? These are some of the less dramatic (and more classified) sides of war, but important nonetheless.

In the hectic first days that followed the government's decision to send a force south, there was naturally a considerable scramble on at home. The Royal Navy brought out every possible ship from repair and refit, recalled others from the sale/disposal list and recommissioned them, and brought back yet others. Several available new buildings were rushed to completion.

War maintenance reserves were broken open and necessary items moved to the ships. An immense transport plan was put into effect to move stores to the docks. Fuel, ammunition, foul weather gear, artic clothing, radios, and spare parts flowed into ships and units. The longstanding mobilization plans worked, even though many items were received unmanifested, and initially stowed that way.

More of the inevitably necessary en route sorting out of people, equipment, and stores between the various ships than might be realized was actually carried out by helicopter, "cross decking" either at Ascension Island or underway at sea. They alone made the logistics ultimately possible, here.

Ascension Island, a lonely, volcanic pinnacle, only seven miles long by five miles wide, slightly more than halfway to the Falklands, was originally a minor combined British/U.S. base. The British turned it into the major joint forward operating base; it rapidly became the funnel through which all traffic to and from the Falklands moved. Hurried departures from Britain made mandatory a major airlift to Ascension. The task force's lead elements paused at Ascension for some days. *Canberra* remained for two weeks. Equipment and stores that had been hurriedly loaded were sorted out here. Troops exercised ashore and were given firing practice. So were the aircraft. Following units caught up.

Later ships on their way south also used the large fleet anchorage as a stopover. On Ascension, not only were supplies, fuel and ammunition stockpiled, but their onward movement was managed. Reinforcements and replacements were continually staged through.

Ascension's 10,000 foot full length but otherwise inadequate airport (Wideawake, no less) became a vital airhead for all shore-based aircraft operating in support of the fleet. Accustomed to, and manned for only three air movements each week, at the height of the crisis it was handling as many as 350 take-offs and landings each day. More than 5,000 men and 6,000 tons of stores were flown in, mostly headed for the fleet. In addition to passengers and freight, ground personnel serviced all planes operating to the south. The necessary engineering, freight handling, weapon loading and administrative personnel brought the base's strength to over 800 officers and men of all three services within three weeks.

The fundamental importance of Ascension made it a likely target for a clandestine amphibious or audacious air attack. Air defense radar was installed, and two fighter aircraft (initially missile-armed GR3 Harriers, later F-4s) stationed there. A detachment of the RAF Regiment provided ground defence. Seaward defences were provided by a navy guardship and Nimrod patrols of the sea areas out to 400 miles. A number of Argentine merchantmen were detected close to the island; these were shadowed by air and surface units until clear of the area.

Although not an exclusion zone, on 10 May a 100 mile radius terminal control area around Ascension was instituted and formally notified to the appropriate international authorities. This called for prior notification of flights to and from the island, and of overflights, thus assisting air defense as well as control of air traffic.

Farther south a major Tug, Repair, and Logistic Area (TRALA) was established at sea. Apparently at 50″00′South 50″30′West, on the northeastern edge of the exclusion zone, the TRALA was east of, and protected by, the battle group, and well out of reach of most Argentine aircraft. Aside from acting as a receiving, holding, and transfer area, much of the resupply and preliminary battle damage repair work seems to have been carried out here, at sea.

South Georgia was apparently never fully developed as an advanced base. It was too inhospitable and too far, and in the end not needed. But a temporary advanced logistic capability was built up there. Moorings laid at Stromness, Leith, and Grytviken provided well sheltered anchorages where resupply, repair, and personnel transfers not possible or advisable in the TRALA or actually in the combat area could be carried out.

Air support of the task force from Ascension was completely dependent on air-to-air refuelling, and on air dropping at the other end, and was therefore restricted to small, extremely high value cargoes. In performing all refuelling tasks between Britain and the Falklands, RAF Victor tankers alone made this possible, providing continuous and timely support. By early June, air-refuelled Hercules C-130s from Ascension were making regular drops of important supplies—including one parachute lieutenant colonel—to ships in the Falklands area.

In all this, too, the Royal Fleet Auxiliary (RFA)—government owned, merchant navy manned, and Ministry of Defence operated—played its role to the fullest. Surface support of the task force was entirely their problem. Out of the RFA's two dozen merchant-design based, naval operations support-type vessels—military auxiliaries flying a blue ensign, although their officers and crew are technically members of the merchant navy—22 were deployed in support of the task force. The Fleet Auxiliary specialized in carrying out high speed underway refuelling and replenishment, even while zigzagging at night, blacked out beside its "customers." The long distances and the paucity of bases here stretched it to the limit. Despite this the RFA even contributed some experienced personnel to requisitioned/chartered ships, constituting an additional de facto reserve for the navy.

While refuelling and replenishing the Royal Navy at sea is normally a function of the quasi-naval RFA, with the nearest supply base 3,800 miles away from the operating area (except for undeveloped South Georgia), the RFA just could not have been expected to cope alone. The addition of a large number of chartered/requisitioned merchant vessels was, therefore, absolutely essential, to re-store and supply the RFA, either at Ascension, South Georgia, or at sea. Some 45 of the vessels taken up were for this and related tasks.

We know that these ships carried more than 100,000 tons of freight, 9,000 personnel, and 95 assorted aircraft. From Portsmouth and Devonport alone the Ministry of Defence shipped over 30,000 tons of provisions, stores, and ammunition. A total of 100,000 man-months of food plus over a million man-days of combat rations were sent out. So were 180,000 metric tons of fuel per month; there were 420,000 tons of fuel at sea at any one time.

The fleet itself had to be logistically serviced, often underway in combat state. It had to be totally refuelled every three days on the average, and the men had to be provided 600 tons of food and 1,500 tons of fresh water each week, fighting or not. Ammunition and spare parts in large quantities were needed, especially once large scale hostilities had begun. Ashore in the Falklands, there was no usable local food or pure water; every bit of both would have to be brought in. There were no other vital support facilities or resources to call upon. Providing all this was the function of the fleet train.

The principal elements of the fleet train operating at or out of Ascension could reasonably be summarized as follows:

- Fourteen commercial oil tankers. Ten owned by British Petroleum, two Swedish, under contract. They operated a bulk fuel shuttle service, first running from Gibraltar and then Ascension;
- Four seagoing tugs with firefighting and salvage gear;
- Six chartered freighters, including a refrigerator ship, one a Norwegian;
- *Contender Bezant*, loaded with aircraft spares;
- Some or all Royal Fleet Auxiliaries, including at least seven oilers and three ammunition and stores ships. These did not have to be requisitioned, of course.

RFA oiler *Olmeda* refuelled the two carriers and their escorts 93 times during the month of May alone, during which time she provided 30,000 tons of fuel and oil. She was herself replenished five times in that same period.

In the end there was roughly a one-to-one ratio between the combatants and their train, at any one time. Put another way, every combatant required the support of one merchantman per month, operating at these distances, at war. By strong implication, little could have been accomplished without such a train.

Participating in the operation even were two vessels of the Royal Maritime Auxiliary Service (a voluntary reserve): *Goosander* (a mooring and salvage ship) and *Typhoon* (a tug). They were far from home indeed, but were needed, went when called, and performed yeoman service.

Except for the amphibious group there appear to have been assembled few, if any, large convoys. A steady stream of individual ships and small convoys ran to and from Ascension and to the combat area and back, however. Each of the latter had to be escorted en route, and defended while in the area. The escorts were stretched very thin.

Aside from handling second line logistics, large numbers of the merchantmen actually went in with the San Carlos assault force's second wave on the first night. These included *Canberra* and *Norland* (*Canberra* looking like a ''great white whale''), both of which were still off the beachhead at daylight. They were not pulled out until the second day, again under cover of darkness. These ships were subject to constant air attack while off the beachhead, but suffered no significant damage.

Commodore Clapp (Commodore Amphibious Warfare) lay permanently offshore in *Fearless*. He controlled force logistics on the Falklands side from beginning to end. *Fearless'* 36 radio circuits carried as many as 3,500 signals a day.

At San Carlos unloading store ships in the anchorage during daylight was quickly reduced to an absolute minimum. A large land forces base area was built up at Ajax Bay, into which stores were shuttled as soon as landed. Each night, a convoy of supply ships arrived, offloaded for a few hours, and before dawn left for the safety of the open sea.

3 Commando Brigade was accustomed to operating autonomously and practiced in taking with it all its necessary stores. Its table of organization included a logistic regiment which ultimately

provided the structural nucleus for the ashore support of the whole force.

In the anchorage the logistics build-up progressed with painful slowness. Unloading only in darkness drastically reduced the expected flow of supplies. Ships carrying urgently needed equipment were sometimes discovered to be out at sea, and could be brought in with the nightly convoy only after complex signals. Twelve thousand tons of cargo were nonetheless put ashore in the first five days, almost all on landing craft or under helos, without loss. Ultimately, 30,000 tons of stores were landed there.

San Carlos remained the shore logistics base until Stanley fell, after which the base was moved there. Even at Stanley, conditions were primitive; the fleet basically still had to provide its own port facilities, including moorings and lighters. Things were indeed taken back to their basics.

In this operation, containers played no real role, a shock to some. Containerized cargo was just not practicable for the simple reason that there were no container handling facilities at the Falklands end. For dry and refrigerated cargo, everything was breakbulk, palletized or not.

Helicopters continued to play a major role in logistics right until the end. Much of the high value, low weight, and volume "ras-ing" was carried out using VERTREP, underway at sea, anchored at South Georgia, at the TRALA, and in the combat area. Helos proved quicker, simpler, and more flexible than any other means. They were always in short supply.

Only a few of the helicopters could operate over land in the dark, and there were 15 hours of darkness a day. Flights were frequently limited by the severity of the weather, although they often did operate under conditions which in peacetime would have grounded them.

Breakbulk: Cargo discharged individual pieces of packages.

Palletized: Cargo loaded in lots on wooden pallets for easier handling.

Ras-ing: Slang, meaning replenishing underway at sea.

With troop transport and supply the real operational limiting factor ashore right from the start, the loss of three very large Chinook and six smaller Wessex helicopters with *Atlantic Conveyor* presented almost a crisis to the land forces. It would seem that several of the under-utilized shipborne helo flights could have been temporarily detailed ashore to help out. (Sea Kings—the ASW dippers—could not, of course, have been spared for this.) More flexibility and some measure of centralized control would have helped here.

On islands where cross-country going is poor at best, the only road is an unimproved track, and helicopters are in short supply, costal waterborne transport could not but play a major role. The Royal Navy made extensive use of its landing ships and craft (and a salvaged interisland steamer) to move troops and supplies forward, wounded and prisoners to the rear. Landing ships *Sir Galahad* and *Sir Tristram* were heavily attacked and set afire while thus engaged just prior to the final assault on Stanley, *Galahad* being sunk.

Demonstrating the extent of the need, *SS Monsunen,* an elderly Falklands Trading Company coaster normally used to carry sheep, wool, and stores around the islands, pressed into service by Argentina, was forced ashore 23 May with chain and rope around her propeller. Put back into service by Britain, she became the task force's most improbable ship, part of the private navy of 5 Infantry Brigade.

Long supply lines and limited availability of spare parts forced all ships' crews to be self-reliant and encouraged ingenuity. *Invincible* remained operational while her engine room staff replaced a gas turbine. On *Avenger* divers successfully changed a propeller at sea. *Hermes'* engineers had to carry out a full boiler cleaning while underway on station in bad weather.

Recent design has emphasized modularization, and unit replacement. Replacement parts were not always immediately available and defective parts were, therefore, repaired on board, often underway, as in the old days. Gas turbines did cause some unexpected problems. Lack of maintenance history left ships' engineers unable to cut corners when time was short, or to take intelligent calculated risks. Engineers required sufficient technical information to allow them to be both selective when doing preventive maintenance and inventive when dealing with operational defects and battle damage.

With the task force operating so far from dockyard assistance, even much major maintenance and repair work had to be carried out afloat, in very rough seas. Achievements of the requisitioned civilian-manned, makeshift maintenance and salvage ship *Stena Seaspread* and of her 100 Royal Navy technicians working in this role were beyond expectations and almost beyond praise. Ships were returned to duty within days.

Before we leave logistics, the medical side of things deserves a few words. Medical attention was given to casualties of both sides, often under fire and in the most squalid conditions. First aid matched the professional expertise of the field and afloat medical teams. Casualties were generally evacuated at once, by helicopter, and in surgery at Ajax Bay within six hours or less. They were transferred to *Uganda* (the hospital ship) as soon as possible. Those British not returned to duty, once fit for further travel, were put on one of the three smaller casualty ferries (*Hydra, Hecla,* and *Hecate*) and taken to Montevideo. There they were evacuated onward to home by RAF VC-10 transports being used for aeromedical evacuation. Over 90 percent survived.

Following the San Carlos landing, the hospital and three ambulance ships were moved from the TRALA to a newly designated Red Cross box, another area of ocean that moved in steps toward the Falklands as the war progressed. In the final stages, *Uganda* anchored in Grantham Bay each day, moving out to sea for safety at night.

By the end of the campaign, British forces had taken a total of 11,400 prisoners of war. The operational situation and the climate combined to increase the considerable difficulties in handling so many prisoners, especially given the shortage of buildings of any kind on the islands and the loss of tentage on *Atlantic Conveyor*. Nonetheless, all prisoners did receive adequate food, clothing, and medical care. Many of the prisoners had, in the end, to be accommodated on troopers, afloat.

Finally, the campaign brought home the contribution that civil resources must make in a crisis, and the value of popular support. The dockyards, ports, and stores depots, together with hundreds of industrial firms large and small, all played a major part in despatching and sustaining the task force. Rail systems and road haulage firms reacted rapidly to move vast quantities of stores and equipment to the docks. More could not have been asked, or given.

So a corporate logistics czar managed the overall tri-service logistic effort. A force was mobilized, manned, stored, ammunitioned, and fuelled, in time, and sent to war. Halfway, Ascension acted as advanced base. Farther south, a TRALA was established at sea. A fleet train was assembled, successfully providing combatants with all the traditional sinews of war. At the force level, anyway, there were no major supply shortages because of the system. Medical care was given; POWs were provided for. Despite the inevitable stresses of battle, the logistics system worked.

WHITE ENSIGN, RED DUSTER

Perhaps 58 merchant vessels of all kinds, from the trans-Atlantic liner *Queen Elizabeth 2* to the tug *Yorkshireman* to deep sea fishing trawlers, were either requisitioned by the navy (28) or chartered by the British government (30) during the crisis from 33 companies. Officially 54 (673,000 GRT) were retained for supply, repair, minesweeping, trooping, or as auxiliary combatants. Once again the continuing necessity for, and flexibility of, an adequate merchant fleet as an element of sea power, as reinforcement for the regular (standing) navy, was clearly demonstrated.

This operation could not have been mounted without the wholehearted cooperation of the Department of Trade, the shipowners, the masters, and their crews. Where there were legal complications (where ships were to be kept on, or extensively rebuilt, or owners/operators would otherwise have been liable for nonperformance of their normal voyages, for instance), ships were not chartered but requisitioned.

Requisitioned or chartered, compensation for ship owners was to be the same. Based on Britain's "Compensation (Defence) Act of 1939," owners were to be paid generous bareboat charter rates plus operating costs (including insurance and maintenance) and the expense of damage repairs or full current value if the ship was lost. Compensation for loss of normal business for up to six months was also allowed. Financial terms were not settled or even agreed upon until the fighting was over.

The mobilization of these merchant vessels was, like much else in Operation Corporate, brilliant improvisation at relatively low staff levels. An Order in Council under the Royal Prerogative, authorizing requisition of any British flag ship and her contents anywhere, was signed by the Queen on the evening of 4 April and announced in Parliament the following day. Freed from financial constraints and red tape, a captain in the Admiralty's Division of Naval Operations and Trade brought most of the ships together merely through a series of telephone calls to various shipowners in a matter of hours.

Many of the "ships taken up from trade (STUFT)" to support the RFA and administered by them in this period never became part of the fleet train. Some did not in fact sail with the fleet to the Falklands. They remained in service, however, sailing home waters, replenishing bases whose supplies were run down in the rush of fitting out the fleet. Others were used to ferry fuel and supplies as far as Ascension. Some even took supplies as far as South Georgia, where a large temporary advanced logistic (supply and repair) capability was to be built up, although no "third party" interest ships are likely to have gone south of Ascension. Others were taken up after the surrender. Numbers are somewhat difficult to pin down, here too.

Geestport, a 7,730 ton freezer ship taken up 7 May, was typical of those from trade, selected for her speed. Her conversion at HM Dockyard Portsmouth consisted of providing a vertical replenishment (VERTREP) helicopter platform on the poop, replenishment at sea (RAS) stumpmasts at four points on the foredeck, a completely rebuilt radio room, and accommodations to take a reinforced crew. She was equipped with additional communications, navigational and cryptographic equipment; nonslip deck paint; extra firefighting gear; extra fork-lifts and battery chargers; as well as a fresh water plant, pump, and issuing rig. Last, she acquired a 24-strong naval party to assist the regular crew to work the ship in her new role: an RFA second officer, first radio officer, bos'n, four radiomen, and seventeen naval storekeepers to manage the cargo. While all this was going on, the ship was loaded with a vast amount of general stores, everything from paint through toilet paper to chicken legs and photocopying paper.

Geestport sailed on 21 May, arriving off South Georgia 11 June. Her basic task in the South Atlantic was to replenish the RFA stores ships so that they in turn could return to the battle area to RAS the combat ships. *Geestport* usually achieved this by going alongside the RFA while she was at anchor and then using the cranes to transfer the required stores. VERTREP was utilized to issue small amounts of stores, and for receiving empties and backloading return stores, a vital task. For other transfers to the shore and other ships, anything that floated was used, even the lifeboats. In all, she made nearly 60 individual issues before returning home on 19 August.

SS *Uganda,* a school cruise ship, was taken up from trade and fitted out as a hospital ship in Gibraltar dockyard. Accommodation for the treatment of up to 300 casualties was provided, together with sufficient medical personnel to cover all major specialties. In accordance with the Geneva Convention, she was declared to the International Red Cross, and appropriately marked.

As has already been mentioned, aside from general second-line logistics support operations, in the fleet train or backing it up, a surprisingly large proportion of the requisitioned merchant vessels actually accompanied the navy all the way, tactically fully integrated into the fighting fleet. They participated in every major operation in both combat and quasi-combat roles. The navy took good care of them. In all the melee, everywhere, only one merchant-man (*Atlantic Conveyor*) was ever lost, and that happened only after her protecting destroyer (*Coventry*) was herself sunk.

Two of the larger requisititioned vessels (*Conveyor* and *Atlantic Causeway*) were Arapahoed, given naval communications and RAS gear, at least two 40mm guns, and an assortment of cargo as ballast, one in nine, the other in eight very hectic days. Carrying a senior naval officer (an RN captain in one case, a commander in the other) and party, in addition to their regular master and crew, they were quickly turned into merchant aircraft carriers ("minicarriers"), effectively units of the fleet.

Arapaho is a new Anglo-American concept. Implying much more than just adding a VERTREP pad, Arapaho provides merchant shipping with individual VSTOL and helicopter capability. It consists of prepackaged and modularized sets of standard freight containers (for quarters, messing, fuel, munitions, maintenance and operations) which can be mounted in various flexible combinations, depending on the aircraft to be supported, on container vessels and, with modifications, on ro-ro vessels and tankers; a landing pad or deck; and a variable but necessarily limited number of aircraft. It can be made to order (literally) for this kind of situation, rapidly installed and similarly removed. More on this later.

Atlantic Conveyor (until sunk) was actively utilized as an auxiliary ferry, a support aircraft carrier. She was, in fact, loaded with Harriers, giant Chinook and Wessex helicopters, fuel, spares, and parts (as well as pierced steel planking for airstrips, and tents). She took on Harriers and other helicopters, carrying them on deck overnight, ready for transfer to the regular carriers in the morning for operations. It is reported that she survived a remarkably long time after being hit, but took with her all except the Harriers and one of her helicopters (a Chinook) when she finally went down.

Elk (5,460 GRT), the ro-ro ferry, was fitted with two 40mm Bofors guns forward and was adapted to house three Sea King ASW helicopters. The helos used her upper deck as a landing pad. She was then loaded with heavy engineering equipment, ammunition and tanks which, since she could not be beached, she eventually must have delivered across San Carlos pier.

Most other merchantmen (the liners, for example) were simply fitted with helicopter pads permitting personnel and material "cross decking" at sea. Nearly all were fitted to refuel at sea. Several civilian tankers were converted to act as fleet oilers. Many were especially equipped with Inmarsat satellite telecommunications terminals.

Average time to alter or add accommodations, communications, helo pads, and refuelling at sea gear was 72 hours for 95 percent of the work in each ship. The majority were fitted and under way within one week.

In the Falklands campaign, large, fast trooping liners—*Queen Elizabeth 2* (67,100 GRT) and *Canberra* (44,800 GRT) being the best known—once again came into their own. While today we all tend to think first of aircraft for moving troops, here the nearest usable airfield was on Ascension. A rudimentary strip could have been cut on South Georgia once it was retaken but even that would have taken an inordinate amount of time. Air transport was of comparatively little use here. Troopers were the only large scale answer. It is questionable, anyway, whether under any conditions aircraft could have carried so many, in such good condition, so far so fast. Only liners can act as hospital or accommodation ships, or carry a floating reserve, ready on call.

Canberra was efficiently and rapidly converted for Falklands duty at Southampton, where she was immediately stripped of her most unnecessary fragile and expensive fittings—chandeliers, curtains, and so on. Those that could not be removed were provided the best possible protection, insofar as that could be done. Two helicopter pads were added, as were the usual underway refuelling and additional communications gear.

Only minimum conversion was attempted. *Canberra* could have carried many (three to four times) more than the 2,000 troops she in fact lifted. She carried that many passengers, but any more extensive conversion would have held her up too long beyond the 48 hours actually needed for what was done.

As *Canberra*'s basic conversion was being completed, additional stores were taken on board. Thirty nurses also came aboard, ready to turn *Canberra* into a hospital ship once her troops and military cargo were ashore (she never was). Many of the regular civilian crew volunteered to stay with their ship; to complete her complement, and to carry out additional military tasks, necessary naval personnel were added. She departed one day late, informally designated a landing ship luxury liner (LSLL).

The last of *Canberra*'s conversion was actually completed en route to Freetown (Sierra Leone), where she put in for refuelling ten days later. It was there that the last of the dockyard workers, who had been retained on board to finish the forward flight deck, were landed for return home.

Queen Elizabeth 2 (*QE2*) took only ten days to convert into a trooper for her thirty day military tour in the South Atlantic. This included installation of the requisite (in her case) three helicopter pads. Some 640 of the 1,040 person crew volunteered to remain on board. This included the master, who was given a naval advisor and who was in constant touch with London. En route, *QE 2* steamed at 26 knots, without an armed escort Once she reached the combat zone, she operated without lights or radar to avoid detection by Argentine submarines.

QE 2 was apparently not used just as a trooping liner, but as accommodation for a floating reserve, standing off from the Falklands, ready to disembark her troops when needed. *QE 2* finally off-loaded her embarked 3,500 man infantry brigade at South Georgia, where they were transferred to two smaller troopers—*Canberra* and *Norland* (13,000 GRT)—and to landing ships and moved to San Carlos. From there the troops marched, helicoptered, and ferried forward into the battle area.

QE 2 was spotted twice by Soviet intelligence gathering vessels, but managed to keep out of reach of Argentine reconnaissance planes. For *QE 2* the primary difficulty turned out to be navigational, from Antarctic icebergs and dense fog (although the fog helped hide her). She suffered no damage, but care was taken on her return to give her a thorough two month overhaul and refit.

All was not beer and skittles, nonetheless. These were improvisations, remember. The majority of assault troops landing from the liners, going in to the beach on conventional landing craft, apparently boarded them over the side, using cargo nets. Climbing down nets hand over hand into boats bouncing alongside, especially in cold, dark, and rain, is slow and uncomfortable at best and dangerous at worst, both for the men and the ships carrying them.

Of all the vessels requisitioned by the British for actual service in the crisis, only the deep sea fishing trawlers (minesweepers) had their entire civilian crews replaced with naval personnel. Many sailed with mixed crews, like the *QE 2*. When *Conveyor* went down, she took with her the merchant navy master and a mix of 11 either Cunard, Royal Navy, or Royal Fleet Auxiliary men. Many of the Chinese and Indian crew members were replaced for political reasons.

The Royal Navy could not have so successfully fought the campaign without its having been able to draw instantly on an extensive merchant navy for all sorts of vessels and crews. The availability of these ships and crews needs to be known well beforehand and their integration must be planned beforehand for them to be mobilized as quickly as they were in this effort. Valid contingency plans and a truly ready reserve are a must. Today an unready reserve is a contradiction in terms.

The British merchant navy has so far never failed to do its part in any of the Crown's many wars. It is an important commercial as well as defense asset. Nearly every conceivable merchant type has a role (other than its normal one) to play in time of war. But the merchant navy too is drawing down, from fifty million deadweight tons five years ago to perhaps half that now. Every day there are fewer of the famous "red dusters," many "flagging out" to flags of convenience (or "necessity," as the case may be). The fall in size has been particularly marked in just those types most needed in war.

At present only ships flying the red duster are regarded as British for defense needs, and are therefore liable to government control in war. However, with many British-owned ships now flying flags of convenience, it would seem sensible if not absolutely necessary now to extend the government's emergency authority to cover all British-owned ships no matter what the flag, as does the United States.

Red duster: *The British merchant navy's red ensign. The Royal Navy flies a white ensign; other government vessels fly a blue one.*

Flagging out: *Transferring registration, usually to a flag of convenience.*

Flag of convenience: *The flag of a foreign, economically more advantageous country, often Liberia or Panama.*

In another war, just how many merchantmen would again be required for absorption into the navy as auxiliaries? What kinds? How many would actually be needed for military support? How many to sustain defense production? How many to keep the minimum civilian economy going?

There is a minimum tonnage below which the British flag, or at least British-owned merchant navy, cannot be allowed to fall if it is still to meet Britain's essential national defense requirements. There must be enough vessels of the right types under British control with available British crews. Evidently the minimum has not yet been reached. That tonnage will have to be determined, and that minimum maintained by whatever means.

MERCHANT AUXILIARIES

Supply ("bullets, beans, and black oil"), including underway replenishment, repair, minesweeping, trooping and even employment as auxiliary combatants, are not unusual wartime activities for merchantmen. Think of Britain's famed auxiliary cruisers on northern blockade and patroling sea lanes in both world wars! What was new in the Falklands was the intensity of merchant involvement at all levels as well as the combat use of commercial vessels as auxiliary aircraft carriers and assault ships. If anything, this traditional interdependence is bound to grow, not become less.

No one should feel that the Royal/Merchant Navy synergism evidenced in the Falklands is unique, either just to the British (the Argentines also utilized merchant tankers as oilers), or the Falklands, or even just for now. With Western navies all becoming more expensive, they will all inevitably become smaller, more intensely combatant oriented. More and more, regular navies will spend the more or less fixed available monies to acquire their ever fewer, higher tech/higher cost fighting ships. Not by administrative default but deliberately, all else will have to be improvised, drawn from merchant assets.

Modern weapons systems provide the means to easily mount very heavy offensive and defensive firepower on a merchant hull.

Harpoon and Exocet can be fired from their own shipping boxes, mounted almost anywhere. Arapaho conversions will gain in importance, both to build up fleet ASW and for self-defense. So will meaningful defensive armament, such as Sea Sparrow, Seawolf and the Seaguard or Phalanx close-in weapon systems (CIWS). The British have come up with a compact version of Seawolf mounted in standard containers, like Arapaho. Phalanx is designed for rapid installation as a modular unit.

Using standard containers, a whole series of weapons systems, radar and sonar equipment, communications, and ASW could be stockpiled, ready to be loaded, bolted, welded, or whatever is required, converting merchantmen in about two days. This would enable these ships to sail armed however and to whatever degree is deemed necessary for their intended role.

We will, therefore, see the level of merchant involvement in naval duties steadily rise. The regular navy will, of course, remain sea power's cutting edge, but that edge will be considerably thinner than it once was. There will be more and more integration of merchant vessels into fighting fleets in time of emergency for logistic support, just as here, and in an ever larger number of quasi-combat roles. The navy/merchant marine distinctions will increasingly disappear, as there develops essentially one integrated seagoing fleet, in peace as well as war.

For this a price will indeed be paid. More and more, combat and merchant ships will have to expect to share in all of the inevitable calculated risks of combat. The *Sir Tristram/Sir Galahad* affair (8 June) is a case in point. It too had been a chance deliberately taken for reasons considered adequate at the time. The last serious Argentine attack on shipping had taken place on 6 June, a raid by two Canberras (one was destroyed, the other fled). Ammunition carrier *Elk* had even been brought into San Carlos during daylight, despite her sensitive cargo. The navy had been successfully unloading at Teal Inlet for a week. Weighing the apparent risk at Fitzroy against the pressing need to move troops forward, two lightly armed RFAs were sent up without escort. What happened then will happen again.

Merchant crews were paid danger money—technically, a war risk differential. For normal commercial crews, this bonus amounted to 150 percent above their regular wages while at Ascension or farther south. Injury and death benefits were also paid. For RFA (civil service) crews, however, the combat zone only extended 200 miles out from the Falklands and South Georgia. Where crews were mixed, as they often were, trouble inevitably arose over these differences in pay.

Although one month or less in a shipyard would turn a fast container ship, tanker, or ro-ro vessel into a dangerous, powerful auxiliary cruiser, with antiship and antiaircraft missiles, and VSTOL or helicopters for reconnaissance, capable for the first time in years of taking on regular combatants, this role is no longer a likely one. Most modifications will remain for purposes of self-defense while providing logistic support to the navy and moving military cargoes.

In the Falklands campaign, still, using this technique, a selected few vessels were converted in just days into auxiliary aircraft carriers, for ASW and other support, of course, and into assault ships, as we know. LASH ships could easily be made into assault landing ships, requiring little or no conversion, although apparently none were so used here. The possibilities are many, and they will be exploited.

Not only will those miscellaneous merchant vessels available in the normal free course of events be considered for taking up, but overt construction and operating subsidies, cargo preference and reservation, tax relief, and other government intervention will guarantee that an established minimum of the right types remains within reach. Such intervention could be expensive, but it is often a choice between this or building up the naval auxiliary fleet to meet whatever comes along. This costs less.

One of the principal lessons to be learned from the Falklands affair is how much and how cheaply both the United Kingdom and the United States could benefit from these merchant auxiliaries. Using ready Arapaho to create just two more "minicarriers," the Royal

---

LASH: *Lighter aboard ship vessel, carrying its own self launching/recovery barges.*

Navy could have doubled the numbers of Harriers that could be supported, for something like one-twentieth of the cost of two of the new *Invincibles*, or less than one-fiftieth that of a medium carrier.

A warning again seems in order. Lest anyone get the wrong idea, improvised merchant minicarriers can never fully replace a minimum core of regular naval aircraft carriers. Minis totally lack the extensive command, control, communications, and intelligence capabilities of a regular carrier. C3I is more of a determinant of success than mere numbers of aircraft, especially in full scale warfare. As useful as minis are, they can only really fill an auxiliary support and escort role. The same caveat applies to all merchant-based types.

Considering the almost certain wartime shortage of escorts of any kind, the increasing use of helicopters to prosecute submarine contacts at a distance from their surface platforms (escorts less and less fight themselves, more and more fight their ASW helos), the sure absence of adequate mobilization time, and the development of the easily mounted (in standard containers) towed sonar array, yet another combat role could be opening up. Consideration in naval circles could also be given to support of a numerous class of small (2,600–3,000 ton), moderately fast (convoy speed plus a little) commercial freighters specifically intended for emergency conversion to the escort role. They would have to carry a helo platform and some defensive armament. They could admittedly only be committed in low threat areas. Peacetime coastal and short sea traders, they would probably have to be subsidized. But they could effectively relieve much of the expected wartime light escort shortage at no great cost. One condition of the subsidy could be an option to take up the ships for a period each year for exercises.

All very well, inevitable even. But a whole new basket of eels is being opened up. The Western world's carefully built up distinction between navy and merchant marine has led to freer commerce and a large body of law protecting merchant vessels in both peace and war. "Freedom of the seas" was sacred, and as long as it did not work against their immediate interests, generally defended by all leading maritime powers. No longer. Unrestricted submarine warfare has to a large extent already vitiated much of this law. The decline of traditional maritime states and the balkanization of the world combine to further erode the law. Present trends with regard to merchantmen should tend to finish off much of what remains of this law.

Unarmed merchant vessels are, of course, extremely vulnerable at any time. They are vulnerable to quasi-official (or official) shoreside noncooperation and obstructionism. They can be immobilized by strikes and sabotage. They are easy victims of all kinds of terrorism. They are subject to all types of visit and search, and exposed in "paper" blockades. They are torpedoed, shelled, boarded, bombed, and strafed. This can only get worse.

From now on, everywhere, in peace or war both internal security on and external security of vessels will have to be tightened up. So will continuing government oversight. These assets are becoming too important to be lost by default.

Merchant vessels are especially exposed while trading in troubled seas during the continuing interim between peace and war. Aside from increased awareness of the requirement for them as merchant auxiliaries, normal questions of self-defense ought to make a capability for rapidly arming them even at distant bases or at sea a matter of priority.

There is, therefore, a strong need to incorporate a number of military-related capabilities into the generality of suitable merchant vessels during time of peace without unduly upsetting what is left of their protected legal status. Among these modifications are helicopter pads; if necessary, they too can be prefabricated and stored ashore pending use. Other items include chaff projectors, for diverting missiles, and underway replenishment/refueling gear. On selected ships, decks can be strengthened for guns, as we used to do.

In early modern English (and, therefore, U.S.) history, there was originally little distinction between the Royal Navy and the merchant navy. In England all through the Middle Ages, the term "navy" did not apply only to the King's ships, or only to the fighting ships. It was employed loosely to cover all ships of any kind

---

Paper blockades: *Blockades declared without sufficient ships to make them effective, therefore illegal.*

flying English flags which could be mobilized by the sovereign in time of crisis. The King not only built ships of his own, he even gave subsidies from time to time to merchants who would build them. Ships were ships, chartered for fighting when need be. Thus "navy" equated to the entire seagoing resources of the realm.

It was the Tudor kings who began the modern differentiation and specialization of seagoing assets, first ordering purpose-built warships. The Tudors still had organized no fighting navy as a separate service. A fully-developed regular (standing) navy with a professional officer corps did not appear until Stuart times. It would seem that we have begun in some measure today to return full circle, at the lower end of the naval spectrum, anyway.

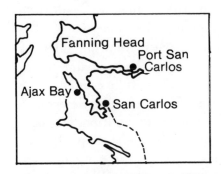

8
The
Necessary
Audit

All very interesting, but where does this take us? War is the final auditor of navies, true. The British won, didn't they? Yet under today's political, military, and economic conditions, a navy must have a firm grasp of its strategic and political responsibilities and a definite plan for its future. Anything less results in unnecessary or even exhorbitant costs for what is accomplished, or strategic and political paralysis in the face of actual challenges, or defeat. Also true. Contradictions eventually surface, every time.

The Falklands war offers the British such an audit, and gives us Americans the opportunity for an easier alternative: another long overdue, relatively painless, real world proxy self-audit. How can either of us turn a blind eye? In the ordinary nature of things, unfortunately, the victors in any conflict tend not to learn as much as the losers.

Here the weather, terrain, and the likely requirement to land away from established ports were similar to the conditions British forces would face in Norway, on NATO's northern flank. This fact alone would compel a certain amount of attention. This much attention the campaign already does get. Much more is needed.

Ships and even fleets can be built with just determination, money and time, but functioning navies cannot. Corporate naval experience, transmitted and reinforced by an honored tradition, cannot be built up without war. The Argentine navy had no even remotely recent combat history and no practical knowledge of conducting large sustained operations on the high seas. The Royal Navy possessed all of the above, and the difference showed. However, there were fundamental shortfalls; they were mostly in the material area but should not, therefore, be ignored.

Naval leaders everywhere can learn much from the Falklands campaign, and so can their political masters. The campaign was an inspired improvisation, force projection successfully carried out by an essentially almost unbalanced sea control and deterrence, alliance oriented fleet. A high seas projection operation, fought in often tumultuous waters at the end of an 8,000 mile supply line, on the fringe of Argentine land-based air power, the campaign was thus in many aspects unique. But there are universal lessons to be drawn, and those tend to be the ones with long term validity.

As we have indicated in the beginning and as the Falklands has again shown, command of the sea is the result of an interacting three element equation, one factor representing the surface of the sea, another the air above it, and a third, its depths. What happens in one element strongly affects and is affected by the other two. Here, the Royal Navy was the stronger (largely by default) only on the surface. It never totally closed off the islands nor did it exercise any clear underwater control. Air superiority remained in dispute until the end.

Air or submarine superiority can and has, of course, on occasion nullified much of surface power. But a dominant surface fleet with however much air, AAW, and ASW is sufficient to offset the major air and submarine threats it faces, remains the primary organ of sea control and force projection. VSTOL and missiles here provided just enough such capability. As real life has shown, redressing the sea power equation's air balance is now a lot more practicable than has been in the past. This, too, should get attention.

Not only Britain but many other nations have interests outside home waters far wider than those covered by regional treaties, as here. There they may have to stand alone. Allies united by regional agreements may not have the same common interest beyond the bounds of that treaty (*vide* NATO). As a superpower, the United States naturally possesses worldwide interests, and may often have to stand alone.

Like all improvisations, the Falklands campaign cost more than it needed to, and more than it would have if it had been properly prepared for. Britain's margin of victory was very small. It must be said, it was a wonder the British were able even just to survive down there, much less emerge so clearly the victors. The Falklands ate severely into Britain's last North Atlantic ASW resources, and most if not all of the losses will have to be replaced. The United States has temporarily taken up the NATO slack, but it cannot do so indefinitely, and should not be expected to. What kind of replacement should there be? What if anything should be added? Does the Royal Navy any longer have recognized conventional war functions beyond convoy and ASW? What kind of a navy should there be in the end?

Military spending decisions cast long shadows over future years. Many fiscal choices are foreclosed for a decade ahead. Today's decisions must lead to a balanced and necessary investment of scarce budget dollars. Major weapons systems today require long lead times; they take many more years to conceive, develop, and build from scratch. A carrier can take the whole decade, for example; a totally new idea, twice that long. Once built, these systems must be manned, operated, and maintained. Decisions once made are difficult to alter, administratively, technically, and politically. Therefore, they almost inevitably harden the navy's mix of ships and planes for the foreseeable future, even in the face of rapidly changing technology and a perhaps uncertain strategic outlook.

In an era where every Western government is having trouble supporting a way of life, providing expected social services, modernizing its infrastructure, maintaining and expanding its productive plant, investing in industrial research and development, and keeping up a prudent defensive posture all at the same time, under normal conditions the amount and proportion of monies devoted to naval forces is going to be severely limited and definitely too little. That is a given. Any recommendations we develop will have to recognize this, too.

The present British government, continuing a long term trend begun under previous both Troy and Labor administrations, has been trimming and restructuring the once well-balanced general purpose Royal Navy. It is again cutting the number of its North Atlantic escorts, scrapping the last of its large deck aircraft carriers, drawing down its amphibious ships and craft, and shifting large funds (perhaps £13.5 billion or more) into a Trident nuclear missile submarine building program. Does this really match means to ends?

In the North Atlantic, NATO and the Warsaw Pact directly face off. Here the fate of Western Europe will one day be decided. Since the Soviet Union here is patently aimed at sea denial, not full command of the sea, the Soviet's surface navy does not consititute the principal danger. Rather, it is their missile and torpedo-launching submarine navy and their air launched missiles that we have most to guard against. These would attempt to sever the North Atlantic lifeline, across which NATO would have to deliver the 1.5 million troops and 28 million tons of weapons, fuel and other supplies required to sustain NATO in the first six months of a central (major European) war. In this time the first allied convoys would have to be assembled, loaded, convoys made up, and escorts provided. Only then could the convoys be dispatched. The first ships (perhaps 600) would have to arrive within 30 days or there would be no point in going at all.

To at least hinder Soviet northern fleet submarines and aircraft from breaking into the Atlantic, the sea passage south between Greenland, Iceland, and the United Kingdom (the GIUK Gap) must be blocked and northern Norway defended. Only by levying a substantial toll here can there be any hope at all of defending the Atlantic convoys. The principal offensive effort in the Norwegian Sea is entrusted to the U.S. Navy's carrier battle groups. The defensive effort—the actual blocking, convoy escort, and support operations—rests with the Royal Navy and other Western European forces.

Sea denial: The denial to an opponent of the use of the ocean, without necessarily being able to use it oneself. Sea denial can lead to command but may not.

The NATO navies would no doubt prefer to carry out these tasks in sequence, first successfully blocking the GIUK Gap, and reinforcing northern Norway, and only then pushing their convoys across. It is not likely that they will be allowed such an orderly approach to their tasks. The strength of the Red Navy and the constraints of time will together prevent it. Everything will have to happen at the same time, with conditions at their grimmest.

Maritime defense here calls primarily for ASW and AAW aspects of sea control carried out by small (escort) carriers, destroyers, and frigates, maritime patrol aircraft, submarines, and mines. NATO navies would have to hunt and kill the submarines, shoot down the missile launching aircraft, and escort cargo ships across in convoys, as before in both world wars. It is for these familiar tasks as well as for strategic deterrence that the Royal Navy, perhaps unduly preoccupied with the NATO threat and the single scenario, has now been structured.

The escort team—surface escorts, submarines, helicopters, and patrol aircraft—is still centered around the surface platform. It is here that the officer in tactical command rides. Recent technological advances have enormously increased the range and speed at which escort actions are fought. Surface escorts now carry long range antiair, antiship, and ASW sensors and weapons, powerful way beyond their size. Using the most sophisticated electronics, the escorts can gather and exploit threat information from many other sources as well as their own improved sensors, and act effectively on it.

As has been suggested, the largest threat to surface escorts today is the low flying aircraft and the cruise missile. The best defense against aircraft is to neutralize their bases, sink their carriers, or failing that, to shoot them down at a distance. The best defense against missiles is to attack, to destroy their air, surface, and subsurface launching platforms before the missiles are fired. Once a missile is released, it becomes very difficult—and therefore costly—to deal with.

Sea control: *The control of a specified, limited sea area, usually only for a limited period of time, enabling one to accomplish a given task; temporary, and local, it may or may not lead to command.*

Countering this threat demandssensors with a reach beyond the typical surface escort's 20 mile sonar/radar horizon.

A naval E-2C AWACS can survey a 238,000 square mile area. It can automatically track hundreds of targets against any background, land or sea, even in the face of ECM, and never mix them up. It can monitor ships at sea down to patrol boat in size. With its passive detection system, it can locate and identify enemy radars to maximum line of sight ranges. Its normal detection range of up to 250 miles and from the surface to 100,000 feet extends air warning and reaction time to 30 minutes. This all gives an AWACS controller time to alert and manage the forces to counter any threat, to vector fighter and attack aircraft or ships to their most efficient intercept position, and gives the fleet a chance to upgrade its own area and point defense readiness to maximum. E-2Cs were designed to be carrier-borne.

Integrating heavy, very long range shore-based E-3A Boeing 707-type AWACS aircraft as well as the smaller navy E-2Cs into the surveillance and control task can extend a naval force's horizon out to 600 miles. E-3As cannot operate from aircraft carriers.

After that, local naval defense against low flying aircraft and aircraft-launched cruise missiles is three-tiered, organized in depth. First, fighter planes flying from carriers, operating farthest out, would attempt to knock down the attack plane or the bomber before it can launch its missiles. Second, surface escorts would employ their own antiair missile against any aircraft that escaped or missiles that are launched, providing area (long range) and point (short range) defense. Third, ships would bring their close-in weapon systems (CIWS) into action, to stop any planes or missiles that succeed in penetrating the outer defenses.

Out of the blocking, escort, and support aspects of this critical sea control task emerged the concept of the small VSTOL/helicopter carrier, capable of accommodating large ASW helos and VSTOL strike aircraft, and also providing the elaborate command, control, communications, and intelligence (C3I) equipment required to manage an active mix of aircraft and ships over a wide area. The strike aircraft were a late addition, carried to protect the carrier and its helos from hostile reconnaissance and attack.

The "defended lane" concept seems for escorts today to be the best operational answer to the antiship missile-armed submarine. Under this concept, a mix of ASW paralleling a convoy keeps a moving passive sonar watch in sea areas on either side of the route being transmitted by the convoy; the depth and sides of the defended lane being a greater distance (250 miles?) from the track of the convoy than the effective range of known enemy submarine-launched antiship missiles (200 miles?).

A close escort using active sonar usually also accompanies the convoy, as still the best answer to the torpedo-armed submarine, although on occasion single or even small groups of large, fast merchantmen might attempt a dash without close escort using only the defended lanes.

Britain normally provides 70 percent of NATO surface units available in the Eastern Atlantic. Recent cuts in the already thinly stretched naval budget would reduce Britain's destroyer and frigate force by about 30 percent. Falkland losses only aggravate an already bad sea control situation. Although Britain is adding a total of three *Invincible*-class VSTOL carriers, like Alice, running fast just keeps us in place.

In Eastern Atlantic waters, direct defense of shipping remains an absolute necessity, especially in the crowded areas nearest Europe. All our exercise and wargame experience tells us that more fighter aircraft, frigates, and ASW helicopters are required. In units of only one or two, as long as the frigates and helicopters have air support, they are effective even in the narrow seas.

Force projection depends on all of the above capability plus an ability to blockade, mine, shell, bomb, rocket, and/or land, support, and supply troops overseas. It demands a variety of specialized amphibious warfare ships, and their escorts, now at their minimum for any really credible British intervention capability. And, ordinarily, it calls for large deck carriers able to provide high performance fighter cover for operations within a hostile air environment, AWACS, and airborne electronic countermeasures. The Royal Navy no longer has these carriers and apparently does not intend to build more.

Force projection will more and more have to be carried out in the face of growing dominance of coastal waters by land-based aircraft, by small, fast (and expendable) surface patrol craft, and by submarines, all of them armed with guided missiles as well as guns, torpedoes, and mines. Projection will become proportionately risky, especially as this sophisticated antiship technology proliferates into the Third World. A navy's room for maneuver, for makeshift and pyramided second-best solutions will continue to shrink, approaching zero.

In the Falklands, if the British had had proper conventional organic tactical air at sea, with an AWACS early warning equivalent to pick up the potential airborne launching platforms out at 200 miles, they would have been able to deal with most if not all of those Argentine platforms long before they could ever have had a fire control solution to launch their missiles. VSTOL and helicopters could not provide this. A medium carrier was desperately needed, to provide the necessary organic air.

But lacking that (or even with it, since some platforms and missiles will always get through), surface vessels must be prepared to defend themselves, of course. A multitiered increasingly dense antiair and antimissile defense in depth is an absolutely inescapable surface requirement. Sea Dart and Seawolf, as good as they were, were just not enough for this job. Losses were severe. They could have been less.

What was missing on the escorts as on all surface vessels in the Falklands was a good self-contained individual final defence. Studies had shown one would be needed, and several were on the market. Here the need was demonstrated. Today this kind of defense equates to a gun-based, radar-directed, small caliber (20–30mm), high fire volume, quick response close-in weapon system (CIWS). Vulcan/Phalanx, for instance, a "bolt-on" self-contained radar on mount-controlled, 20mm point defence system capable of 3,000 rounds/minute is just such a weapon. So is Seaguard.

Organic air: *Aircraft and air units organizationally integral, included as a regular part of the fleet.*

It has been held that a navy has four possible functions in society. In order of priority, these functions are:

- Internal security ("aid to the civil power");
- Defense of the homeland and its possessions (common to all);
- Support of international defense commitments (like NATO); and
- Other support of foreign policy.

Sea power is the means by which these are accomplished. Only command of the sea can guarantee them.

Only a force based on surface ships now can accomplish all this with a 24 hour/365 day, high volume, long endurance and range, all weather capability, against any enemy. They attack other ships and defend their own. They carry troops and supplies. They provide gunfire support. They provide the absolutely essential command, control, communications, and intelligence. Ships are the ASW and AAW screen. Neither planes nor submarines can yet substitute for them, although the newer weapons are certainly necessary adjuncts to any navy's continued full exercise of power at sea.

Neither internal security nor aid to the civil power was, of course, in question in the Falklands. Defence of a dependency, even though "out of area," was the question (who could be more British than the "kelpers"?), along with overtones of foreign policy support. Execution of this second priority function with the resources at hand was a very close thing. Should it have been risked so closely? The fundamental decision is, of course, a political one. Once made it is very difficult to alter.

The Royal Navy's fixation on its NATO role almost to the exclusion of all else was, of course, forced on it over the years. So was the shrunken surface force. This strategic preoccupation, over-specialization, and paucity of resources has, nonetheless, led to a steady erosion of that inherent flexibility that is one of the prime characteristics of properly developed sea power. Either the navy's responsibilities or its future plans should be brought into line before worse takes place.

REDUCING THE COST

The following discussion summarizes what might be the principal useful lessons of the Falklands fray and interpret them for the future, with specific reference to Britain, Argentina, and the United States. In the Falklands the British paid a severe price for their fine victory. It is for them that the most direct conclusions can be drawn. We shall, therefore, begin with them. Argentine and U.S.-directed comments follow.

As experience now shows VSTOL attack aircraft and helicopters do provide a fleet with some effective measure of organic air capability in distant seas. As long as its ships carried landing pads, VSTOL and helicopters could do so even for a fleet without carriers. Just two small VSTOL/helicopter carriers significantly expanded a fleet's capability here. Without them the Falklands could not have been run.

For the VSTOL Sea Harriers, is strengthening the wings and adding fittings to carry increased external fuel, giving greater range, and increasing the armament from two to four Sidewinders enough? More and more, VSTOL are being flown in the short take off, vertical landing mode, materially increasing (by perhaps 2,000 lbs.) their otherwise very small potential load. But are they really sufficient for a force projection of this intensity? No, not if any more extensive solution is available. It appears that at least one is.

Can the newly developed, British helicopter-borne AEW (airborne early warning) radar really substitute for an AWACS? Equipment and crew limits, normal helicopter vibration, lack of range and endurance all say no. Britain's margin of victory in the Falklands was too slim not to demand an order of magnitude better for the future.

This study must be preliminary and its conclusions tentative. Again, we are not instructing the Admiralty, and this study should not clash with any of the official positions that must have already been taken by the Admiralty. It is certainly not intended to. The study really ought to support them and assist them in presenting some of their case to the Treasury and others.

Britain does, no matter what, face a searching naval self-audit. In future campaigns of a similar nature, it does seem that the Falklands price could in fact be materially reduced. The key problems of long range surveillance, of truly adequate air cover, of low flying aircraft and standoff surface-skimming antiship missiles, and the related need for an effective close-in air defense system are not impossible of solution. There are at least three principal British naval options.

The Carrier Option

One or more medium (30-40,000 ton) conventional fleet carriers, with two catapults (or one catapult and a ski-jump ramp), arresting gear, a landing system, and an angled deck large enough to support a respectable number (around 40) of high performance fighters, mini-AWACS-type airborne early warning and electronic countermeasures planes, and a mix of other aircraft should be used. The *Invincible* (and *Ark Royal* or *Illustrious*) type of small or light (16,000 ton) carrier/VSTOL/helicopter combination is excellent for ASW and escort aspects of sea control operations (which is what it was designed for, and for which it certainly should be kept), but less than optimum for other tasks. It is too small for most force projection scenarios. Neither VSTOL nor rotary wing aircraft are presently able to provide the lift necessary for true fighters and AWACS substitutes, especially the early warning craft, and small carriers can support nothing else. No truly acceptable alternative to the medium carrier, therefore, yet exists, and none is expected to become viable in the immediate future.[*]

As carriers are usually the largest and most spacious ships in their task forces, they are usually required also as flagships. They must, therefore, expect to have to provide operational spaces and accommodation for a flag officer and his staff, and communications, something that none of the alternatives can do at all. The *Invincibles* are especially equipped with command facilities for maritime air operations.

---

[*]The only aircraft that could possibly assume a full AWACS role for the Royal Navy under these conditions before the end of this decade would be the Bell XV-15 or some similar tilt rotor or tilt wing.

A minimum of two carriers should always be available for deployment at short notice. To ensure this, a third carrier should be regularly maintained in refit or reserve. One at least should be a medium conventional type.

The Nimrod Option

Nimrod maritime patrol aircraft (Mk-3) should be fitted out not only for AWACS but also themselves flexibly armed. The versatile Nimrod is normally credited with an endurance of about 12 hours and a radius of somewhere around 2,800 miles. Nimrods operating from Ascension using inflight refuelling effectively doubled this time in the air. All carried their normal ASW ordnance. Some at least were armed with Sidewinder air-to-air missiles for self defense. Some carried air-to-surface versions of the U.S. Harpoon missile. There seems no unsurmountable reason why air-to-surface antiship missiles could not regularly be carried, or why all three types of ordnance could not also be. The Soviet Union has managed successfully to achieve it. The Nimrods, like all aircraft, are load limited and will require adequate shore bases within operational range. This solution has the virtues of being "state of the art" and reasonably cheap.

Alternatively, Nimrod aircraft could be fitted only to carry out the full AWACS function, combined still with aircraft from existing small VSTOL carriers. However, the Nimrods will still require shore bases within operational range, and dependence on shortlegged (if superb) Harrier types as fighters will continue. Although undoubtedly an improvement over what exists, and cheap, this could only be second best.

Nimrod aircraft could also be fitted out not only for AWACS, but also for directing the fire of offensive/defensive missiles launched from surface platforms. In tomorrow's battles naval technocrats at airborne consoles will more and more decide which ships are sunk and which planes and missiles are shot down. Although effectively circumventing the inherent inability of AWACS-fitted Nimrods to carry very much additional ordnance, or of VSTOL to range far enough to really defend against modern planes and missiles, this is obviously a high tech second generation solution, still far in the future.

Unfortunately, as things are now, for Nimrods actually to operate over the Falklands, with the nearest usable base 3,800 miles or so away, a flight of over 16 hours would have been required just to get there and back, plus inflight refueling time. Time on station would have been limited by crew fatigue, if nothing else. To maintain one Nimrod constantly on patrol would have tied up about eight all told, to say nothing of a quite considerable number of tanker aircraft as well. Evidently, in any maritime conflict beyond easy range of shore, it now would be dangerous to rely on any airborne early warning other than that organic to the fleet itself.

Without adopting at least one of these two general approaches— medium carriers (now the best) or Nimrods in some configuration or other (looking to the future)—and appropriate tactics, effective long range maritime surveillance and adequate air cover does not seem within reach. And on this all really significant improvement in British operational capability depends.

A CIWS

Since some platforms, some aircraft, and some missiles will always get through the best area defense, a more widely distributed close-in defense against aircraft and antiship missiles should be incorporated to include a rapid firing, gun-based CIWS. There must be a CIWS. Total reliance for close-in defense cannot be placed even on a good short range anti-air missile system. A CIWS is a goalkeeper, complementing the missile system. Phalanx and Seaguard are already off-the-shelf items. No ship being sent into harm's way will last long without them from now on.

Sea Dart (and Seawolf) have to be fine-tuned, and the now apparent bugs worked out. They could do much better than they did. Too often outweighing the ability of one or even two frigates to protect another ship against air attack was the risk that escorts took as additional targets.

The Falklands finished forever the idea of aluminum superstructures on naval vessels. Originally conceived to reduce topside weight, aluminum was found to melt and to burn too easily. Damaged British Type 21 frigates (the *Amazons*) suffered badly from fire. Under intense heat, their superstructures tended to become molten masses of metal, making damage control operations virtually impossible. All signs are of an immediate return to steel (or Kevlar). The U.S. Navy had already made this decision, although it will be years before the last aluminum is gone.

Also, too many of the materials used in British ship construction were unnecessarily flammable. Some (PVC covering for cables, for instance) also gave off clouds of extremely dense, black, acrid smoke and toxic fumes when hot. So did some of the furniture. Change is indicated here, too. Firefighting equipment must keep pace.

Urgent studies are now in hand to improve survivability, both of existing ships and future designs. Examples of measures that reportedly will be taken include less flammable material, improved fire zones, better watertight doors and hatches, more escape hatches, better smoke-tight bulkheads, relocated fuel tanks, additional fire pumps, breathing apparatus, and personal breathing sets. Not a moment too soon.

Ideally then, each major surface escort should have at least a general purpose missile launcher, a CIWS, a large caliber gun, and a helicopter pad, as well as a complete air, surface, and subsurface sensor array and ECM/ESM. She will have to carry extensive communications, especially for intrateam contact. Some more internal system redundancy and more ruggedness would seem to be in order.

There are still other gaps in the British naval force projection arsenal even though they did not happen to appear in the Falklands operation. The Royal Navy lacks a heavy air-to-surface antiship missile, for example. The contract for the Sea Eagle antiship missile was only very recently awarded, and was then very nearly axed as part of the latest defense cuts. This, too, will have to figure in future trade-offs.

Both effective political control and military command of this operation required good communications between London and the task force. Here the vital importance of satellite communications in operations conducted at great distance and in areas notoriously bad for radio propagation was clearly shown. A dedicated military satellite and terminals in all major men o'war is also called for.

Electronic warfare—pick up and identification of targets and appropriate action (to blind, confuse, divert, or destroy) against them before those targets get you—is here to stay, too. The British in the Falklands could listen to the enemy's radar and tell from them where he was and what he was doing. They could also jam enemy radar, blanking the screens, or feed them with false signals. They thought they could throw most Argentine missiles off course. Communications between the Falklands and the mainland could be jammed. Reportedly, in the Falklands British-built radars were easy to deal with, the U.S.-built ones somewhat harder. Flares and chaff continue to play a role.

Still, U.S. carrier-borne EA-6B tactical jamming aircraft are capable of electronically hiding an entire carrier task force, effectively shielding it against long range bombers and cruise missiles. At the same time, they can provide safer approaches for our own strike planes. This too should be (again) looked at.

As things stand now, in the spring of 1983, it will soon be almost impossible for the British to mount another such Falklands operation. In time, the necessary ships and expertise will be irretrievably gone. What actually are the Royal Navy's responsibilities then to be? Is Britain in fact to become only a regional naval power, able to concentrate on limited nuclear deterrence, on Western Europe and the Eastern North Atlantic? Or does it still recognize vital, unilateral, purely national and "out of area" worldwide interests, including shipping and trade, that it also wants to defend?

Britain's almost unanimous national response to the Falklands crisis tends to indicate that there are still such interests. If this is

---

Chaff: *is a package of small, thin strips of aluminum, fired by rockets to form a cloud. Radars are deceived into treating the cloud as a target, and missiles are seduced away accordingly. Chaff is an effective passive defense, given sufficient time.*

Flares: *are fired to decoy heat-seeking missiles.*

so, current plans for the Royal Navy urgently require some immediate, serious retailoring, and we now have some at least tentative guidelines to indicate how this probably will have to be done. The Royal Navy is not too small nor are the threats it faces too one-sided or overwhelming for it to undertake such a task.

There will be costs here too. There will still have to be trade-offs. But these costs are reasonable, and the tradeoffs need not always be between naval conventional war forces. Why should the navy have to carry the whole burden of the strategic missile replacement program by itself? If it must, the British might then have to give up a Trident submarine or two, or just stick with their present Polaris types altogether, and acquire a new medium carrier or two instead.

In short, reducing the cost of like campaigns boils down in material terms for Britain to rebuilding a balanced, flexible, general purpose navy in the sense that term is understood today. The solution is ready at hand. The trends are clear. So are the options. No study alone could have pointed them out as well as this war. The only real unresolved question here would appear to be the proportion of disposable resources to be devoted to near term issues (carriers, and so on) as against long-term ones (Nimrods?).

The antiship air and missile threat demands near-instantaneous aircraft, ship, or force reaction times. This translates easily into automated responses by complex weapons and strange black boxes. But skilled tactical commanders remain keyed, keeping their ship or plane or force ready for the threat, prepared to change tactics to meet innovations introduced by the enemy. There is no escape from that for anybody.

9
The Armada Republica Argentina

Much of what has been written and said here about the 1982 Falklands/Malvina affair deals with events through British eyes for a number of reasons. A word about the Argentines, their navy, their great air force, and their army seems in order. While the Argentine surface navy (*Armada Republica Argentina*) alone was overall only about one-third the size of the Royal Navy (about half the strength of the British task force), it was a balanced, relatively modern, and efficient regional force. What happened to it? There is much to learn here, too.

Historically structured to provide a counterbalance to that of Brazil and a margin of superiority over that of Chile, at the opening of hostilities, the *Armada* numbered one carrier, one cruiser, nine destroyers (two of them British-designed Type 42s), five frigates or corvettes, and four submarines. Included were demonstrably adequate sea-lift and amphibious assault capacity, in the shape of two landing ships and six transports. It was backed by far superior air power, including a small organic naval air arm. The carrier, the cruiser and seven of the destroyers were aging, but all had been updated with missiles and modern radars. Not all of the ships, however, were to prove operationally ready.

The *Armada*'s naval air arm itself entered the conflict as a sizeable force. It included three attack squadrons, one ASW squadron, one reconnaissance squadron, two helicopter squadrons, two logistic squadrons, and one training squadron. They were all well-trained and up to date. Airborne refuelling was widely practised. They were ready.

The *Armada* here had but one real task: seize, occupy, support, and defend the Falkland Islands, It also had convenient nearby bases at Puerto Belgrano, Trelew, Comodoro Rivadavia, Santa Cruz, Rio Gallegos, Rio Grande, Ushuaia, and elsewhere from which to operate. It was not too seriously inferior to the original British task force and with adequate air support should have been able to give a good account of itself.

Answers as to what happened to the *Armada* should be of special interest to the whole maritime world, not just to smaller navies. Even supernavies cannot be superior everywhere, everytime. Elements of even the strongest fleet occasionally have to go on the defensive, fighting from inferior positions. This is more difficult. What has been found out about what took place tends only to support the old strategic truths.

For the Argentines the solution to the Falklands problem at every stage depended on command of the sea. That took sea power, of course. The Argentine navy, however, could not ever have solved that problem by itself. It lacked a sufficient air arm of its own. It is, therefore, difficult to consider just the navy alone, in isolation, although some relevant comments can be made. The air force keeps intruding, but sea power is based on a navy. It was the key.

In the Falklands the Argentines appear to have been content at first just to maneuver for strategic position, as in a game of chess. A battle would almost have been regarded as evidence of clumsiness or stupidity. Exercising a local and, as it proved, temporary command of the sea, they seized a designated limited, easily isolated objective—island territory geographically distant from a homeland—stuffing it with troops and then going on the defensive. This set up a situation where it should have been more trouble for Britain to turf them out than the prize was worth. It was the traditional pattern of small maritime wars, soon settled at small cost.

The British confounded their plans by making them fight. Argentina may be said to have had initial control of the sea and air around the Falklands, but their navy soon abandoned its command of the sea, and their local command of the air degenerated into an intermittently continuous melee with no one in clear control. Forcing them to fight seems to have somehow paralyzed them, in a strategic sense.

The commander of the Argentine navy is reported to have publicly stated repeatedly that the principal function of his navy was defense of the homeland. Since in this situation the mainland was not threatened—the political need to keep the war limited and the paucity of British resources combined to ensure this—that left little for his navy to do. Next after the mainland must have come defense of Argentina's integral new province, *las Malvinas*. It was his clear duty. His navy's justification was in his hands.

As we have seen, the *Armada* precipitated this war with occupation of the Malvinas and the Georgias del Sur. This occupation represented a neatly executed maximum (largely administrative) effort on the navy's part. The *Armada*'s subsequent effort can be conveniently divided into three distinct phases.

The First Phase

Beginning 5 April, the Argentine navy was extensively regrouped and restored, preparing to defend its new gains. The whole of the major combat and support units was redesignated Task Force 79. After an intense period of individual training and checking of its equipment, between April 15 and 17 this force sailed from Puerto Belgrano, this time headed for intensive target practice and antisubmarine (ASW) exercises. On 27 April the fleet deployed to its assigned operating areas southwest and northwest of the Malvinas, ready to counter an attack against either the mainland or the Malvinas.

During this phase, also, the navy ran a series of exercises using their modern British-built Type 42 destroyers to establish and publicize the ships' capabilities and weaknesses. This paid off handsomely later.

The first phase then saw the combat elements of the Argentine navy grouped into two parts: (1) a main force (TGs 79.1 and .2) that included their carrier (*25 de Mayo*, conventional but roughly equivalent to Britain's *Hermes*) and her escorts, and the bulk of the destroyers, each group with an oiler, deployed to the east of Golfo San Jorge, approximately 300 miles off their coast and 150 miles north of the Falklands, covering both the mainland and islands; and (2) a smaller force (TG 79.3) which included the cruiser, two destroyers, and an oiler deployed southwest of the islands, covering the Straits of Magellan and Cape Horn. By 29 April, they were positioned to commence operations.

This phase ended as *General Belgrano* was torpedoed just off the southern coast, and *Santa Fe* was attacked and run around off South Georgia. *Sheffield* was sunk in exchange. The show of force indeed was over.

The Second Phase

Reconnaissance from the carrier (U.S.-built S-2s) finally located lead elements of the British fleet on 1 May, some 300 miles to the northeast of the main Argentine force, moving south. This initiated the second phase. *25 de Mayo* closed toward the enemy at 20 knots, planning to launch an air strike at dawn. The launch never came off. The Argentine main force kept the British fleet some 100 miles to their north and east for two days—apparently without being discovered—still attempting to launch a strike against them. One story is that the weather (fog and lack of sufficient wind) combined with the carrier's slow speed precluded her A-5s from being able to take off with a load sufficient to make an inevitably expensive strike worthwhile.

To await better weather the Argentine main force was finally ordered to withdraw to the continental shelf on 4 May. Probably the rumored presence in the area of British nuclear-powered submarines and an unfortunate assumption that the enemy was now able to count on satellite information concerning the position and movements of the *Armada* (making impossible any further large scale surface maneuvering or other tactical surprise against his surface units) also had something to do with this. On the continental shelf at least the water was considered too shallow for British submarines to operate safely.

The Third Phase

From then on, up to the end of the conflict, the Argentine surface navy operated along the mainland coast on ASW missions such as maritime surveillance, defense of the ports and their approaches, and other vital coastal targets, as well as electronic warfare tasks. Auxiliary units contributed to transportation and resupply and performed search and rescue. The brunt of what remaining fighting the *Armada* did now devolved upon its naval air arm, its submarines, its marines, and the naval personnnel in the Malvinas.

The *Armada*'s air arm as a whole did well, anyway. They alone among the air elements had the appropriate airborne munitions and the techniques for delivering them. In this final phase, the carrier's aircraft were all landed and dispersed to shore bases, mostly opposite the islands, from which they participated in the overall air effort. Once there, better trained and equipped for operations over water, they got more than their share of kills.

The MB-339 Aeromacchi-equipped 1st Aeronaval Attack Squadron was transferred to Puerto Argentino (Stanley), where it flew under operational control of the Malvinas commander. The 2nd (Super Etendards) and the 3rd (A-4s from the carrier) were located at Rio Grande on the mainland, remaining under operational control of Commander, Naval Air Command.

It was a naval Aeromacchi flying an armed reconnaissance from Stanley that confirmed news of the British landing at San Carlos. Further air strikes were immediately called in, from the mainland as well as Stanley. The Super Etendard squadron sank *Sheffield* and *Conveyor*. The A-4 and the Macchi squadrons accounted for *Ardent* and *Antelope*. A P-2 vectored the Etendard onto *Sheffield*. Transport aircraft flew into the islands up to the last day.

Reportedly Argentine naval aircraft losses were moderate (three A-4s, five Macchis, and others). More than half of the planes lost were destroyed on the ground through enemy action. Only four naval air arm pilots were lost.

Submarines, like aircraft, are a natural weapon of defending navies. Argentina's four submarines should have done better than they did. The story of *Santa Fe* we know. The second of the old U.S.-built submarines, *Santiago del Estero*, was never operational during the war.

Operating in familiar waters at close range, the *Armada*'s two German-built Type 209 diesel submarines should have posed a considerable threat to the task force. With British submarines held beyond the 12 mile limit (by reason of their deep draft as well as by order) there should on paper have been no reason why these small, quiet, and maneuverable boats should not have been able to break out to sea at will. They did get out at least once but as we know accomplished little.

Salta, one of the two modern Type 209s, did begin an operational patrol but soon returned to port, accomplishing nothing. The other, *San Luis*, was apparrently well commanded but sank nothing; what happened to her wire-guided torpedoes we do not know at this writing, and may not ever.

On the Malvinas, the 5th Marine Battalion reportedly fought well, integrated into Stanley's land defenses as a tactical reserve. It was a lone naval officer and two civilian technicians who in ten days out there put together a makeshift Exocet coastal defense battery, the one that finally hit *Glamorgan* 30 kilometers away.

The Argentine surface navy remained withdrawn, and apparently played little further significant role even in the crisis battles. Although considering its air support it was not seriously inferior to the British task force, and did include old but still operational and effective *25 de Mayo* whose quite powerful air group and its contingent of A-4s had a 400 mile radius of action (as against the Harrier's 100 mile radius), it does not appear to have been sent out again to fight. There have been rumors that the carrier had engine trouble, but in any event the loss of *General Belgrano* and *Santa Fe* early on may have effectively discouraged the Argentines from seriously committing any other major combatants where they would be at risk.

As far as is known, it must also be said, once Argentine fleet units pulled out of the Falklands, the British-declared Falklands maritime exclusion zone was never seriously challenged by the navy, nor was the (paper) Argentine blockade effectively enforced. Neither British submarines nor satellites totally ruled this out.

The principle is, a navy too weak to win and keep command of the sea by large scale offensive operations but still possessing secure bases may yet be employed so as to hold the issue in dispute.

It carefully avoids actions likely to lead to its complete defeat, and assumes an active defense, tying down enemy ships and preventing their use elsewhere. Such an approach in itself cannot lead to victory at sea, but even over prolonged periods it can prevent an opponent from engaging in major offensive operations or otherwise exploiting the sea. It gives the defender time to dominate the situation by somehow securing his ends ashore.

An active defense thus disputes another's control of the sea through a strong tactical offense. It attempts to keep a stronger opponent off balance, preventing him from enjoying the full fruits of superiority, keeping him from exercising control by sorties against his naval force and/or raids on his maritime communications, requiring counteraction, tying up his assets.

Admiral Anaya should have been able to disperse his offensive assets all along his mainland coast, forming scattered small task units. Always assuming adequate air cover, these task units could have broken out east by night, randomly, to stage (or even just threaten) hit and run Exocet raids against the enemy. Anaya would inevitably have lost some ships, perhaps to those British submarines, but he could not let the unlucky prospect of heavy losses deter him. Here there were no feints, no actual sorties, and no raids, not even against a British line of communication that paralleled the Argentine coast for the last 900 miles.

Without what he considered adequate ASW forces, Anaya apparently felt *25 de Mayo*'s task group could not risk lengthy maneuvering against British units.

The Argentine fleet had two possible primary main force targets: the carrier group and the amphibious group. The key to this operation patently was the two carriers (*Hermes* and *Invincible*) on which British operations were based, (shades of Midway!). If the Argentines sank or disabled even one of them, they had the amphibious group in their hand. In this they never succeeded, although aircraft at least searched repeatedly for the carriers and did succeed in sinking another of the carrier task group (*Conveyor*).

Then, on the first days at San Carlos the pilots went for the escorts and not for the vulnerable and more immediately vital amphibious ships and transports. Sinking enough of the amphibious ships might have stopped the British; the escorts could be replaced, the amphibious ships and troops not. Instead, the pilots engaged in a mutually destructive duel with the escorts, and the landing continued.

Had the Argentine surface fleet presented even a hint of an active threat, the resulting defensive precautions would have tied up significant amounts of limited British resources, indeed. Pressure on the *Armada* to do something, however futile, must have been great. The Royal Navy would probably have won any major clash at sea, but only a partial victory would have changed little and even the threat of a clash would have greatly complicated British plans. Any resulting pause in British operations could, in view of the coming winter weather, have indefinitely delayed their assault.

The Argentines could always have hoped to draw perhaps only a part of the Royal Navy into battle under circumstances disadvantageous to the British but maximizing their own strengths (air power), thereby defeating the British in detail. Such naval battles have to be planned. Naval forces must be used in such a way and positioned in such places that the enemy will be compelled to fight if he intends to make any effective use of his own forces. The chances of this succeeding did exist, but they were slim.

Or, Buenos Aires could have tried to wear the British down to manageable size through attrition. On the face of it, they did try it. Success here would depend in part on the possession of superior weapons (Etendard/Exocet) and in part on the coming winter weather. It would also take time, which the British did not allow them.

Once the *Armada* had carried out the invasion, it had the task of somehow protecting the garrison and denying shipping approach routes to any liberating British seaborne forces. Minefields were a logical choice. The navy duly laid a number of conventional moored contact fields, some blocking anticipated offshore approaches (near the outer entrance to Port Stanley, in fairly deep water, for example), others as barriers protecting vulnerable shore installations subject to attack. None seem to have been laid off San Carlos.

The *Armada* had taken a considerable interest in unconventional underwater warfare (midget submarines, frogmen, limpet mines, and the like). Although the Falklands campaign should have offered a variety of opportunities for this often effective kind of operation, there is no record that any such unconventional effort was ever made.

There have been several suggestions that *General Belgrano* would have been better employed as a "fortress ship," anchored in Port Stanley (like *Canopus* in 1914). There her fifteen 6 inch guns would have added immeasurably to the defense, and there was a good chance that most if not all of her guns could have been served even if she was sunk, and resting upright on the shallow botton.

Such employment of *Belgrano* as a fortress ship must be weighed against the impact she would have had "crossing the T" against a possible hostile force exiting the eastern end of the Strait of Magellan (as did Rear Admiral Jesse Oldendorf's old battleships at Leyte in 1944). Anaya opted to prepare for the latter, and lost.

As with naval air arm pilots, there was certainly no shortage of courage among Argentine mariners, either naval or merchant marine. Supply ships continued in their individual attempts to run the British blockade throughout the war. A number reportedly got through, one as far as Stanley only days before the surrender. Others like *Isla de los Estados* inevitably paid the ultimate price for their daring. All defended themselves with vigor, and even impertinence.

The Argentines had a fleet in being at least. A good naval defense meant keeping that fleet active. Only some form of tactical offense could really have justified its existence. There is some evidence that a last death or glory sortie by the surface navy was actually considered in the war's final days, but it never came off. The Argentine navy was held simply as a fleet in being—the least effective of its possible spectrum of roles. Anaya's potentially decisive fleet thus, even in the crisis battles, continued on its minor

---

Crossing the T: *Steaming in a line across the head of an enemy force also in line so as to be able to bring all your fire power to bear on his lead ship or ships while most of his is masked.*

Fleet in being: *A fleet which avoids decisive action but because of its mere existence and location requires constant watching, using up forces which could be utilized elsewhere.*

costal defense tasks—a passive threat which the British still to some extent did have to cover—until the end.

The other decisive Argentine strategic error may have been their failure to fully exploit Port Stanley's short but hard-surface civilian airfield. Properly utilized, the field could have been the key to victory, much as was Henderson field on Guadalcanal in 1942, impervious to torpedoes and almost so to bombs. The airfield's runways were not built to take high performance aircraft. They were always wet. They would have had to be lengthened and strengthened to take such aircraft (and that might have been quite a job, given the island's geology) but the Argentines did have more than three weeks between occupation and the arrival of the British fleet to accomplish it. Once done, this would have given the Argentines a 400 mile reach not just from the mainland and their carrier, but also from Stanley. Nothing in this area was done. The field was used essentially as is, for C-130 transports, Macchis, Pucaras, helicopters, and the like only.

Apparently the Argentines on the Falklands planned a classic mobile defense. They could not defend everything, everywhere, in any case. They retained the bulk of their forces in Stanley, scattering small garrisons around the islands. They had to have planned on support and rapid reinforcement of these outposts by helicopter from Stanley once the main assault was identified.

However, the Argentines soon lost local control of the air. There was no counterattack against the beachhead, and their inexperienced troops stood up only poorly to the isolation, foul weather, and continuous bombardment from the sea. The shock, and confusion generated as the British overran the final defensive positions around Stanley while most of the defenders were still asleep finished them as a coherent fighting force.

Throughout, the Argentines seem to have continued to honor all outstanding international technical agreements. No military operations appear to have taken place south of 60° south latitude, in full accordance with the Antarctic treaty demilitarizing the area. Argentina's Omega radionavigation transmitter remained "on the air, in sync, at full power" all during the crisis. (Omega Argentina is, of course, too near and of little use in the Falklands area itself.)

When all is said and done, what we might have seen in part here could be called the developing navy syndrome. Modern, fully-developed states expect that in a war between good and efficient navies, more or less equally matched, tremendous damage will be reciprocally inflicted. Many ships on both sides will be lost. But for a developing navy that has scrimped and struggled so hard and long to collect its modest horde of beautiful ships, such an idea becomes unbearable. The overwhelming tendency is to conserve these ships, not to risk them. Here would neither be the first nor last instance we see this attitude toward losses, self-defeating though it may be.

Total Argentine losses included ARA *General Belgrano,* ARA *Santa Fe,* ARA *Alferez Sobral,* ARA *Comodoro Somellera,* ARA *Rio Iguazu,* ARA *Islas Malvinas*; and SS/MVs: *Rio Carcarana, Isla de los Estados,* and the fishing vessel *Narwal.*

In the end, the *Armada* did remain essentially intact. The British had neither the time nor need to root it out. With the exception of *General Belgrano* and *Santa Fe,* Argentine fleet losses were minor. Whatever else, the regional balance of naval power was maintained more or less as it originally was. That at least was left.

Such is a watershed in naval history, now seen from both opposing perspectives. In it the basic principles of naval warfare as described by Julian Corbett for one, some time ago, stand essentially as they were.* If anything, the importance of these principles was strengthened. The Argentine experience is especially enlightening. To fully justify its existence, a fleet must remain active, keeping on the tactical, if not the strategic offensive. The penalties for failing to do so have been brought home once again.

Among the unanswerable questions that one finds in the debris of every war, one in this case must be: in light of the fact that the Falklands affair ended such a close-run thing as it did, could not a more active Argentine surface navy at least in the period, say between 21 and 25 May, have spelled the difference between actual defeat and victory? It seems that just might have been the case. The

---

*Julian S. Corbett, *Some Principles of Maritime Strategy* (Annapolis: Naval Institute Press, 1972). The first edition of this book appeared in 1911 in England.

750 to 1,000 Argentine men who died then would not have done so in vain. Wars are to be won.

As the Falklands war most clearly showed, while modern naval warfare has indeed become electronicized—technology battles technology—at sea the decisive importance of informed, skilled, and aggressive leadership is in no way less than it ever was. Here the British had the edge. Since the various other factors in the strategic estimate were so closely balanced, it was the decisive edge.

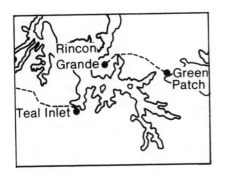

10
The
U.S. Interest

The Falklands war was a matter of very deep interest to the United States, for a variety of immediate reasons, and for the future. We are presently undertaking a naval renaissance, aiming at a 600 ship/15 carrier battle group fleet by 1990. In the Falklands, many of its concepts were combat tested. The North Atlantic Community is a maritime one, occupying the rimlands surrounding the ocean and tied together across it. Its security is ours. Next after the United States, Britain contributes the most to its maritime defense. We had to be concerned, at many levels.

In the Falklands the United States saw two of its good friends fighting, and was forced to choose between them. We could not win on that one. A most strenuous and occasionally even frantic diplomatic attempt was made to avoid the political necessity for such a choice by mediating between the two, but this effort, like all others broke down. The United States then reluctantly announced a formal recognition of its obligations to its oldest and best ally. We imposed full military and economic sanctions on Argentina (most military supplies were already denied; only some $5.9 miliion worth of equipment and parts was affected) and offered material aid to our ally.

Indirectly we were deeply involved here. Let no one think this choice was made lightly. Underlying everything had to be the fundamental requirement that the United States make a choice it could live with. When we could, we had to oppose changes in the world order imposed by force, against the wishes of those most concerned. This choice is not always open to us. The choices in international relations are too often only between two bad alternatives, but here the issue was clear. Argentina was the regretted aggressor. And we could choose.

Immediately Britain's involvement in the Falklands conflict seriously drew down the NATO contribution of the principal naval power in the Eastern Atlantic. Several of the scenarios for a third world war were envisioned, with a Soviet-encouraged diversion in an obscure corner of the globe, taking political attention and military resources away from Europe, and thus offering the Soviets the opportunity for a preemptive strike. The United States had to temporarily fill this shortfall, with assets culled from other areas, as had been mentioned already, our fleet becoming more intensely committed than any time since Vietnam.

Not a lot is said about direct U.S. assistance to the British, still for what should be obvious diplomatic reasons, but it was considerable. A certain amount of fuel was made available on Ascension, as required by earlier agreements. A number of U.S.-built "smart bombs," Shrike antiradiation missiles, additional advanced Sidewinder missiles, and other such items were provided. Some naval communications went through U.S. networks. They may have been getting some signal intelligence and minor satellite data. But there was no direct U.S. involvement.

The United States had long ago acknowledged the need for antimissile defenses and an adequate CIWS. Phalanx had already been developed and was an off-the-shelf item. Phalanxes in fact provided the Royal Navy were mounted on *Illustrious* (the second *Invincible*), for instance, and on *Invincible* herself later, but none as far as is known saw action in the Falklands. We were at least ready on that one. (So is the Soviet Union, by the way).

There is a very reasonable rumor that once the need became clear, the British asked the United States for the loan of a large E-3A AWACS or two, to operate from Ascension. The United States recognized that this loan could be of immense value to the

Falklands task force, saving lives and shortening the war, but reluctantly we here had to refuse, since the AWACS would be of no use without a fully trained crew. The British could not provide this crew, and Washington could not loan one. No American personnel were themselves to fight their other friends.

The United States also must have a deep and abiding professional interest in the naval strategies, tactics, and technologies practiced in the Falklands by both parties. Such a laboratory cannot be simulated, and knowledge in war does save life. It is possible that the United States has both recognized and digested the naval lessons already outlined. The former is probable (official sources of information have to be better than those available to the public), the latter not so probable. We, too, are hypnotized by the single scenario.

It is in the merchant marine area that most remains to be said, and in the carrier versus supercarrier area. The United States also needs to look at what it is doing with honesty and intellectual rigor. Problems there are.

Washington should be able to count on having the following merchant-type assets available to it in time of war, for combatant support and sea lift: (1) the Military Sealift Command-controlled fleet of some 130–140 government owned and chartered ships, presumably always ready; (2) the Maritime Administration (MARAD)'s National Defense Reserve Fleet of about 250 ships supposedly ready to sail within three to eight weeks; (3) the regularly steaming U.S. flag merchant marine of 600 or so commercially owned oceangoing vessels; (4) a 300–400 ship "effectively U.S.-controlled" fleet, flying flags of convenience (many manned by foreign crews, whose enthusiasm for joining a U.S. war must be understandably suspect); and (5) under only certain conditions, assistance from allies.

The United States pays considerable attention to its naval combatants. The combatants listed in the navy's present long range (1990) 600-ship deployable battle force plan will probably be properly and fully funded. It is less probable that monies for all the auxiliaries such as naval oilers and supply ships will also be voted. Historically, this has always been the case. Sounds from Congress indicate it is still so.

To make the most of what monies it has, the navy has begun leasing ("long term bareboat chartering") rather than buying some of its auxiliaries. It even stimulates construction of certain types of vessels, participating in the design stage. These lease arrangements shift part of the real cost of the ships out of the Pentagon budget and push many of the payments 20 or more years into the future. This only enhances the normal naval importance of our merchant marine.

MARAD requires all U.S. flag merchant vessels and certain foreign flag, American-owned merchantmen of 1,000 gross tons and over, engaged in foreign commerce and not operating under control of the Military Sealift Command, to report departures and arrivals, and their at-sea positions every 48 hours. MARAD uses the data to maintain a current plot of these ships as a basis for marshaling them during emergencies of whatever sort.

On the other hand, where merchant-type auxiliaries and sea lift become a governing factor, the United States today is coming perilously close to not being able any longer to achieve its foreign policy objectives by itself, should that become necessary. In 1952 to support the Korean War, only 12 percent of the U.S. flag merchant fleet was called upon. If the United States had to support another such effort now, on the same scale, 80 percent of the fleet would be involved. There is little give left in the overall system, either to provide for the needs of the navy and the civilian economy, or to allow for losses.

Sea lines of communication to Southwest Asia for us stretch 12,000 miles, not even just 8,000 miles as for the British in the Falklands war. Up to several hundred merchantmen might be required at very short notice to support U.S. operations in such distant areas. The necessary types do not all now exist in our operational inventory. Nor do we have sufficient shipyards to perform naval modifications even on a limited scale, especially if such modifications have to be made to several hundred units essentially all at once.

The United States' equivalent of the RFA is the Military Sealift Command (MSC), a Defense Department organization managed for it by the navy. It is MSC that manages the increasing civilian involvement, at least in the lower (logistics) end of the spectrum of peacetime as well as wartime operations evident in the U.S., too. MSC's own expanding fleet—civil service manned—currently contains some 60 ships including oilers, scientific support ships, tugs, ro-ros, cable layers, and stores ships. To these should be added seventy to eighty commercial charters, as needs be.

Fewer and fewer even combat-related tasks are being performed by the navy itself. Under one program, for instance, we are presently acquiring eight 33 knot container ships, converting them to combination ro-ros. After conversion, each of these fast sealift ships will be able to carry as much as 150 C–5 aircraft—a month's airlift to Southwest Asia. They are to be held in readiness for loading on five days notice, and could be loaded in three to four days. Even they, however, would require two weeks to deliver cargoes from the West Coast to Southwest Asia. We are, therefore, also acquiring 13 regular military prepositioning ships, self–sustaining ro–ros designed to offload mixed military cargo in poorly equipped ports or even over the shore. They are to be stationed near potential trouble spots. As part of the program, MSC's civil service-manned ships and commercial charters are both taking the strain. A potential 90–100 vessels could ultimately be involved. So far successful, this is another sign of the times.

There is in the United States also an increasing involvement by the navy's ready personnel reserve in the manning of the Maritime Administration's ready reserve merchant-type auxiliaries and sea lift. The intention is that these specially designated vessels be available five to ten days after an alert. Initially 30 and eventually 70 vessels could be included in this program. The Falklands probably did expedite this.

On the other hand, if what happened in the islands is any gauge, SSs *United States, Constitution,* and *Independence,* with their large troop capacity and great speed would make ideal troopers for our Rapid Deployment Force (RDF), especially where airfields, for whatever reasons, are not available. Communications to Southwest Asia stretch 12,000 miles, remember? *Constitution* and *Independence* are active cruise ships. At present laid up, *United States* could possibly also be required at short notice for trooping. What are the odds of her being as ready as *QE2*? Where are the helicopter pads? Where is the defensive armament? Where is the crew? Could we even approach British readiness?

Even after everything that happened in the Falklands, Arapaho may be in trouble in the United States. Since it is so uncertain exactly what help the navy will be able to provide next time, Arapaho is required here to protect convoys by permitting ASW helicopters and VSTOL strike aircraft to operate from containerized bases aboard merchant ships themselves, if for nothing else.

Arapaho has not really been actively pursued by the navy in the United States, probably because of a combination of strong interlocking bureaucratic reasons. The navy has not come to grips with the command, control, and communication involved in utilization of merchant vessels, and therefore tends to ignore the issue. The navy also fears that Arapaho would compete for funds with regular construction of escorts. Finally, Arapaho having no peacetime value, it generates little active duty navy support.

At $20 million for a full-scale Arapaho set—enough from which to conduct a plausible defense against torpedoes and missiles—a 610 foot container ship can be turned into an auxiliary carrier in just 10 hours. The 12,500 square foot flight deck and 4,000 square foot hanger can easily support 7 helos operating 24 hours a day. Arapaho is cheap (a frigate costs $200 million), it uses existing equipment, and it works. It is being starved for lack of funds.

Several specific recommendations follow from what has just been said: (1) inventory critical navy related merchant assets and keep track of them; (2) plan to utilize Arapahoed ships for ASW (and AAW); (3) prepare the necessary Arapaho kits, and ready the helicopters (and Harriers); (4) prepare the communications, navigational, and cryptologic gear and establish the naval reserve units necessary to solve the merchant auxiliary C3 problem; and (5) train the necessary reserves.

As can be seen, the United States can validate a number of its ideas concerning sea control and force projection as a result of this war. It can even learn a few things about antimissile defences and about mobilization of merchant assets. About its requirement for a balanced mix of aircraft carriers, there will be no consensus. Regularly generating much smoke and little fire, as it does, this last problem deserves further space of its own.

SUPERCARRIERS AND OTHERS

Although not directly involved in the Falklands affair, in the United States it again raised questions concerning the United States' requirement for supercarriers. Serious, informed men of good will differ on the question of the U.S. Navy's need for super-carriers. Even Admiral Hyman Rickover gave the average life ex-pectancy of a supercarrier in an all-out nuclear war as just two days. Exercise "Ocean Venture" (1982) did not settle the matter. Con-troversy continues unabated. Surely the answer depends on the scenario one has in one's head as one answers the question. The issue is a major one and affects not just the United States. Let us see what guidance the Falklands experience offers us here.

Supercarriers are statistically imposing vessels. A thousand or more feet long, they are truly large deck carriers—with angled deck, catapults, and all-weather landing system—easily capable of carrying a mix of 80-100 fixed and rotary wing aircraft including high performance fighters, attack aircraft, AWACS, electronic countermeasures planes, and an ASW element (S-3As and helicopters)—and capable of launching and recovering them at the same time. They carry massive amounts of fuel, munitions, and spares. They make ideal flagships, easily able to provide both com-munications and space. They do have everything. They are ex-ceedingly cost effective where there is an objective requiring their full clout.

What does a supercarrier cost? In gross figures, the ship herself costs perhaps two billion dollars. But that is only the begin-ning. Her air wing adds another billion. Carriers must always have support. Her Aegis escort costs another billion. Three more de-stroyers add up to another billion. This brings the total for an operational supercarrier battle group to approximately five billion dollars each.

Do we, therefore, reserve these superexpensive supercarriers for incidents where, to protect sufficient perceived national interests, it is considered their huge strength is needed and should be risked? Any ship can be sunk. *Bismarck* was. *Yamato* was. Even seemingly minor damage can put a carrier out of action. Any loss or even disablement of a supercarrier would be extremely serious for the larger strategic balance.

Evidently, the survivability of ships cannot be measured in terms of losses alone but in relation to what is achieved. Any platform in a hostile environment is vulnerable to some degree. Each attracts a weight of attack in proportion to the forces an enemy has available and his perception of the threat the ship poses to him. The real question is not whether the ship is vulnerable (which like all weapon systems it is, of course) but whether it is so vulnerable that it cannot perform its tasks.

What then do we do about lesser wars—in the Persian Gulf, say? The navy reportedly refused to station even one of our supercarriers close off the coast of Iran during the hostage crisis (1980) for fear of her being sunk. To avoid risking the precious big carriers, do we in such cases provide no organic air at all?

And what if there occurred two or three different lesser crises—lesser but still seriously involving significant national interests—brewing at the same time? This is not an inconceivable situation, one that might well be generated by an adroit opponent as a preliminary to larger moves elsewhere. Any unplanned diversion of the tightly scheduled supercarriers leaves an unfillable gap in our intended carrier force distribution, and ultimately in our central defense. The even temporary absence of two or three at the same time could be dangerous. What about distributing the risk?

What difference would or could the presence of a single *Nimitz*-type (96,000-ton) supercarrier have made in the Falklands? A proper combat air patrol equipped with air-superiority fighters (F-14s or even F-18s) launched from such a carrier should indeed have prevented the worst of Britain's losses. However, given an always more or less fixed total naval budget, and a reluctance to cut their seabased nuclear deterrent force, there would have had to be fewer of these other ships to start with. Whatever losses the British still took would have been felt that much more keenly, to where an opposed landing could no longer have been a real option.

Our navy justifies its current request for 15 supercarrier groups as necessary in a major war with the Soviet Union. Some supercarriers are certainly mandatory for operations in the higher threat, higher intensity NATO areas (the Norwegian Sea, the Mediterranean) and the northwest Pacific. Superthreats do call for supercarriers. The United States will have to supply these, and in appropriate numbers, but perhaps Admiral Elmo Zumwalt was right. It may be that what U.S. Navy really needs is a carefully thought-out high/low mix of carriers.*

For instance, the United States is presently reactivating four *Iowa*-class battleships. Plans supposedly are that sooner or later we will remove the ships' aft single turrets and add a flight deck on the cleared space. Acquiring these modified *Iowa*s would be roughly equivalent to building four 47,000 ton fast, well-armored, and well-compartmented "battliers" (hybrid battleship-carriers), carrying VSTOL and helicopters, and armed with missiles and six 16 inch guns each. They would be invaluable in force projection situations such as this, for missile and naval gunfire as well as air support, but only if and when they become VSTOL-capable. They cannot operate in a low threat hostile air environment even without some sort of air cover, and they are designed in part to relieve supercarriers, not tie them up.

Patently, not all wars are going to be large, central (NATO-Warsaw Pact) conflicts. There still will be small wars like this—perhaps not as important as but more ugly than this one—where we will once again have to land or withdraw troops against sophisticated opposition outside the range of land-based air cover, where surface-to-air and surface-to-surface missiles are not enough. Some organic air is still an absolute must. In part, the hybrid *Iowa*s reflect such a need.

In a war like this, two (or three) medium (30-40,000 ton) carriers might be operationally often more useful than a single big one, in any case. They could both be had for the price of one *Nimitz*.

---

*"High/low mix" is Admiral Elmo Zumwalt's term.

They would still carry a respectable number of air-superiority fighters and AWACS as well as other aircraft. Two carriers would permit the embarked air wings to arrange a division of labor (day/night or offensive/defensive operations) and relief over extended periods, allow for breakdowns, and acknowledge the ever-present possibility of loss.

From any view it cannot be cost effective (or safe) to swat flies with a sledge hammer, or fight small wars with supercarriers. Just as the British would seem to require one or two medium aircraft carriers to support their small escort carriers, it can be strongly argued, so the United States with its greater spectrum of involvement needs small escort and medium carriers to ease the load on its big carriers. Even the Soviet Union is now busy building medium carriers to back up their VSTOL types, to broaden their capability mix.

So far we have managed to avoid such old chestnuts as, in the world as it is, to be or to be perceived as weak or irresolute is to practically guarantee insult. Or, prevention (deterrence) is cheaper and better than cure. But there they are once again. The three billion dollars that the Falklands campaign cost the British would easily have paid for a medium carrier group, complete with escort. Some 1,000 British killed and wounded would have been avoided, not to mention the three islanders. So much for that.

In the supercarrier controversy, the United States does not usually seem to address the right issue. Smaller carriers do no doubt cost more per carrier per plane per sortie, and the rate does go up as the carrier decreases in size. But smaller carriers do still cost less overall than supercarriers, ship for ship, and these smaller carriers have important roles, as the Falklands experience shows. So do the big ones—there is no quarrel there. The situation, therefore, does not resolve itself into either/or. We need both. The essential question is rather, how many of each do we need?

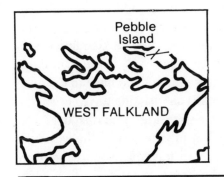

11
Epilogue

Today, in the Falklands, a year after the close of this truly unfortunate war, while on the surface the local political *status quo ante* has now indeed been restored, militarily, things are forever changed. Strategically, effective defense of these distant islands remains a major problem. Only the implied threat next time to bomb mainland Argentine airbases and mine harbors—and the continued presence of a 4,000 man drawn-down British task force—keeps de facto peace. As things stand, no further Anglo-Argentine discussions regarding the future of the bleak, far-off islands are likely soon. London seems stuck with the problem. Let us look at this.

The future political status of the Falklands—within or outside the British Commonwealth—has not yet been worked out. Colonial status could well end, Britian being left responsible only for defense and foreign affairs. Or things could remain as they were. One thing is clear. To any diminution of British sovereignty the staunch kelpers remain unalterably opposed. If anything, their experiences during the war have hardened their original position—three islanders died in the fighting, all women.

Buenos Aires has formally reserved the option of reopening an armed struggle it says is halted but not over. The government appears grimly determined to avenge a humiliating defeat. The *Armada* takes an even stronger position. "The move initiated on April 2, 1982, still has not ended," the navy's present commander Admiral Ruben Franco has said. "The navy has a debt to settle." In a society still (1983) ruled by a military junta, the *Armada*'s own corporate view of the world carries special—in this case ominous—weight. Many Falklanders are convinced that whoever sits in the Casa Rosada will attempt another seizure of the islands sooner or later.

Any hope of a peaceful settlement of the Falklands issue is thus gone until fighting fevers on both sides cool. There is nothing to do politically but wait. Buenos Aires may indeed have to exercise that military option if it really wants these islands anytime soon.

While immediately the struggle was and remains over the Falkland Islands and its dependencies, for the rest of the world, in the longer range view, this could all well have been a precursor of things to come in Antarctica and the South Polar seas. The world could well begin really to need those resources by 1991.

Tactically, the military threat which the rump combined task force still in the islands currently might face should be low, one which the present 4,000-man force could handle easily. Argentina is not likely to renew large scale hostilities in the next few years. It will, however, seek ways to keep the pressure on. From time to time, token Argentine air or commando raids might well take place, creating a maximum of furor. These would keep the issue open politically, at least, while Buenos Aires better prepared the diplomatic ground in the U.N. and elsewhere, for whatever comes next. Uruguay and Brazil are now closed to traffic to and from the islands.

In four months of backbreaking work, engineers have repaired and enlarged the existing Port Stanley airfield so that it can now base F-4 fighter-bombers. This has allowed the navy to bring the task force's last remaining carrier (*Illustrious*, relief for *Invincible*) home. The airfield's new hard surface is regrettably only temporary, good but for a few years. It is ringed by gleaming Rapier batteries.

Communications with home remain almost entirely seabased. Some 30 chartered merchantmen are still engaged full time, supplying the islands, as before, paralleling the Argentine coast for 900 miles. Some 16–20 merchant vessels and warships fill Stanley harbor on any given day. The busiest place in town is the jetty.

At the surrender, a naval boarding party from *Cardiff* took possession of Argentine coastguard patrol boat *Islas Malvinas*, still afloat at Stanley. The prize was refurbished and commissioned into the Royal Navy as a HMS *Tiger Bay*, for use in off-shore patrol. *Bahia Buen Suceso* was also taken over.

Sir Galahad's burned out hulk was towed out to sea, and scuttled. A constructive total loss, *Sir Tristram* was first employed as an accomodation ship, than later towed home for possible rebuild. Two small ro-ros have been chartered as temporary replacements for them.

Ro-ro ferry *St. Edmund* has become HMS *Keren*, with a civilian crew. She is back working the South Atlantic ferry services between Ascension and Stanley, supporting the garrison. There have been other MoD purchases, too.

Container ship *Astronomer* is reportedly going to be fitted with a ski-jump and flight deck for both VSTOL and helos. Also fitted will be containerized vertical launch Seawolf, complete with search and fire control radars. She is formally to test the concept of a self-contained air defense system on continuing runs to and from the islands.

In the long term, most anlysts see the "Fortress Falklands" garrison being reduced to about 2,000 men. About half of these would be ground combat forces (a small reinforced infantry battalion) the remainder being shared between RAF and navy. It is expected that patrol craft and a station ship will remain in the Falklands in addition to *Endurance*. Several frigates, a destroyer and at least one submarine will maintain a presence in South Atlantic waters. There should be a mother ship and other afloat support. Air cover would be provided by a mixed squadron of F-4s and Harriers. There ought also to be a helicopter unit and at least several maritime patrol planes.

There will have to be a lot of military construction work throughout the islands, as they are in effect fortified: surveillance radar stations, artillery and missile emplacements, food, fuel, and ammunition depots, roads, secondary airstrips, naval piers, and the like. A whole military infrastructure will almost have to be created from scratch, much different from and more extensive than that required for a 90-man company of marines, costing some $3 billion over the next three years.

Most important will be the development of the present Stanley airport into a major "strategic" (international) one, extended and strengthened so that it can handle the large, long range transports it would take to reinforce the garrison quickly in a crisis. It must be equipped to fight off a surprise attack from the air. It also must be substantial enough to resist damage or to be repaired quickly if any raiders do damage it. The present London government is committed to this.

To the islanders, all this military activity amounts to a second overwhelming invasion, even if peaceful. It will permanently change the former socioeconomic structure of the islands, modernizing and making it almost completely dependent on the 2,000 military, rather than as previously when it was the other way around. Sheepherding is already on the decline.

This time, however, the garrison itself must be sufficient and credible in the purely tactical sense. The local military balance again has reverted to Argentina. Nonetheless, if trouble did break out again, even one reinforced battalion, a handful of aircraft and surface ships and one submarine should be able to conduct a significant delaying action (more than just making Argentine "eyes water"), buying time until they can be reinforced.

Behind them rests the whole might of Great Britian, already mobilized once in ultimately commanding power even over this extraordinary distance. As long as external political and military conditions do not change, that is, the garrison does not stand alone. That by itself should give Buenos Aires pause. Periodically mounted exercises will demonstrate (and test) Britain's reinforcement capability.

Argentina's *Armada* is nonetheless busy making good its losses. Twenty four A-4s reportedly have been received from Israel, and will be assigned to the navy. More of the Super Etendards already on order in France are arriving, together with their Exocets. Four destroyers, six frigates, and six submarines are also on order, should begin arriving shortly, and are all expected to be in hand by the end of the decade.

Now having been blooded, so to speak, the *Armada* can be presumed to have learned from experience. It ought now to be a much more dangerous combat-ready foe new equipment or no.

Should Argentina move again militarily against the Falklands, it is in any case most likely that this time the war would widen, to include bombing mainland airbases, mining commercial harbors and naval bases, perhaps even instituting a close full blockade. For one thing, Britain simply could not just abandon 2,000 men to their fate; time would be a critical factor and bombing would be both effective and quick. Such a strategic-level response would give them time to get more definitive help to the area.

Chances that we shall ever see the Royal Navy coming back to the islands in the same strength and composition again are low, however. The critical factor is Stanley airfield. As long as the British hold that, there should be no need for another large scale amphibious landing, much less an assault. The fleet that came would therefore be smaller, leaner, more completely a fighting sea/air, blockade oriented one (followed still by its train), ready for the naval battle we still have to see.

In the politico-military sense, the regular presence of such a substantial garrison presents the seemingly still passionately determined but temporarily checked Argentines with a credible and sufficient deterrent. Buenos Aires must believe London will really fight for the islands, as many times as is necessary, at whatever cost. These 2,000 men should be evidence enough of commitment sufficient to perceived interests for them to do so. As long as external conditions do not change, there should be no need to actually prove this point. Many would hope so.

Beyond all this, with force Britain has only really bought time and reopened political opportunity for all sides. Despite now really enormous residual psychological obstacles and undoubted political barriers, further discussions on the islands' future political status—some sort of accommodation between reasonable people—should be possible. These tiny, desolate islands cannot be allowed indefinitely to remain a threatening *casus belli*. The realities of geography remain immutable: the Falklands are 8,000 miles from Britain but only 400 from Argentina.

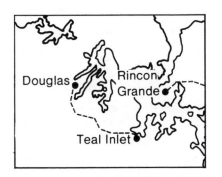

12
Conclusion

Some 18,000 officers and men from the Royal Navy, Royal Marines, naval auxiliaries, and merchant navy sailed in those courageous ships of the Queen's Falklands task force, to fight the Royal Navy's first missile age war. In all, 44 warships were involved, 22 RFAs, and 45 STUFT (50 if one includes the trawlers commissioned as minesweepers). Eventually over 110 ships were for some period deployed south. It was a truly remarkable effort.

Many of the personnel manning these ships were very young, some had never been to sea before. Several ships had already been at sea for months before the operation started. After long periods underway, closed up at high states of readiness, often in very bad weather, they kept their ships, aircraft, and equipment on top line, and then fought hard and well. By the time they returned, many had been continuously at sea for over six months. It was a great achievement, worthy of the best of their past.

The Royal Navy's attention had for years been focused on fending off economizing politicians, on strategic deterrence, and on preparation for the Third Battle of the Atlantic. In some ways the Royal Navy has to look upon the Falklands war as a fortuitous accident. For a navy that has had to fight almost literally for survival against successive governments, Parliament, and the Treasury, the

157

war provided an opportunity to demonstrate a principal reason for being, and its capabilities in this area, just before it was too late.

In some ways, cold-bloodedly, it must be considered as good fortune that the Argentines struck before *Invincible* had been transferred to Australia, or the assault ships *Fearless* and *Intrepid* had been scrapped, or the dockyard "mateys," who because of navy cuts fitted out the Falklands task force with redundancy notices ("pink slips," to Americans) in their pockets, had left. Even so, prodigies of improvisation were called for.

There were three major problems to be overcome: (1) lack of air cover for the British while the Argentines could provide both fighter and attack support from their mainland bases; (2) the enormous logistical problem involved in sailing a fleet 8,000 miles and keeping it supplied so far from its bases; and (3) the coming Antarctic winter, with storms, mountainous seas, and subzero temperatures, including very dangerous windchill factors. Each was dealt with successfully in its turn.

In every war, especially at its beginning, there are von Clausewitz' "frictions." Operations are always beset by indecision, confusion, human error, technical failures, and fate. This was no exception. Planning was hampered by rivalries among the military staff. Operations were plagued by accidents and equipment failures. These frictions were surmounted here through the military school system all shared, tradition, leadership, and bravery.

The British were indeed lucky here, but once again fortune favored the brave. What if Argentine bombs or torpedoes all had worked? What if the Argentines had counterattacked the San Carlos beachhead the day following the landing, using all arms? What if the *Armada* had intervened seriously at any stage?

In this case, also, Her Majesty's use of force has served a useful British political purpose; the political worth of military power has again been validated. At the bottom line, the political *status quo ante* has been restored, the trade-offs are bearable. The Royal Navy had done very well indeed, as everyone knows. Its ships were cheered mightily on their return, too.

In the long run, foreign policy and sea power need each to reflect the other, however. For Britain to continue to depend on such luck alone seems a little ridiculous, if not dangerous. If Britain expects to act again unilaterally "out of area," it had better be ready. Not to be ready—and to be perceived as ready—is just to invite another such war.

To recover these far-off islands, this small war cost the British an estimated $3 billion ($1.2 billion in direct costs), at least six ships, 777 men injured and 255 (174 at sea) dead. Three islanders also died as they were being freed. It left a weakened NATO, even though the gap was temporarily filled by U.S. forces. It left a number of lessons for both Britain and the United States, and the Soviet Union in similar force projection scenarios.

Force may be the last argument of kings, but as the Falklands again showed, any use of force—large or small—today tends automatically to raise the argument to almost unmanageable levels. It compounds the problem of negotiation, foreclosing many political options. Any military defeat is too humiliating. Even naval symbols are too emotive. If employed at all, force would appear in most cases to have more immediate political utility as a defensive symbol than as an offensive one.

In the Falklands, successive minor military escalations just did not convey the right political signals. If *Endurance* had fought until sunk, if Royal Marines had died in the very beginning, the ultimate British response would have been clearer, the Argentines quite possibly more ready to compromise, fewer casualties might have been demanded later. It looked for too long as if overwhelming Argentine *force majeure* faced only a paper lion.

Once battle is joined, sea power, however gained, maintained, and exploited, is in water areas still the *sine qua non* of victory. The Royal Navy's success underlines the continuing importance of balanced flexible maritime forces. That has not changed one bit. Sea power is divisible, however. Command of the Eastern North Atlantic does not necessarily carry over to other sea areas.

What else then have we concluded for the future, useful for any navy? In the Falklands, the Royal Navy faced the most common situation in naval warfare: not even a locally and temporarily commanded sea, but an uncommanded one, with sea control in running dispute. With a reasonable naval force, as has been pointed out, blockade and amphibious assault evidently can still be carried out.

What has changed now is that, as was demonstrated in the Sound, armed with the small carrier/VSTOL/helicopter/missile, surface fleet scan once again operate within a hostile air environment, albeit at some cost.

The war in the Falklands, never formally acknowledged as such, was a truly classic example of carefully contained limited conventional war. Here as always, time was the critical factor for both sides.

The Falklands experience gave added impetus to the idea of integrating shore-based air more closely into the struggle for command of the sea. This idea comes and goes in the West, but underutilized shore-based air is potentially too valuable a tool to be left out of the battle. Coordination has to be by the navy.

The role of submarines—nuclear-powered or not—in the low intensity preliminary phases of conventional war was not settled here, and will be with us for a while. At what point does sinking ships become an end in itself? Why?

Merchant vessels are an integral part of maritime power. They here played and will continue to play an ever larger naval role, coverted quickly to provide military support, with the distinctions between merchant marine and navy increasingly disappearing. Their defensive arming in a hostile environment is vital. No navy is ever going to be large enough or ready enough by itself from now on.

At the technical level, this was perhaps the first really significant high tech/high cost naval war. Computer faced computer. Helicopters were in constant use. Among all of the new weapons employed, the Harrier VSTOL and the Exocet missile stand out. VSTOL and "smart" missiles are here to stay. Aluminum superstructures on naval vessels are not. Antimissile defenses will have to continue to improve. Perhaps not sufficiently acknowledged was the broad technical base required to sustain such a war. Not everyone can really do it.

And, the arguments against only supercarriers, for some medium (and small) carriers, for AWACS, for CIWS, and for large, fast troopers (where one can afford them) have gained somewhat, in Falklands-like scenarios. The Soviet Union may have gotten it right, after all. Their medium carriers are on the ways.

In the light of the unexpectedly high rates of consumption of both ammunition and stores during the campaign the size and composition of the stockpiles intended to support operations both within and outside the NATO area have to be again looked at.

According to the British press, it has been decided that *Hermes* (only until *Ark Royal* is ready), *Invincible, Fearless, Intrepid,* three guided missile destroyers, *Endurance,* and several others scheduled for retirement, are not to be sold, at least for now, and only Chatham will be closed. A three-carrier level will be maintained. Is this reorientation, or only reprieve, again?

As is always the case, good men paid with their lives for these lessons. Tentative though most of the lessons have to be, will we pay sufficient attention, avoiding the shoals, yes, but taking the tide? Will Washington as well as London now better match our naval means to ends? Those who refuse to learn from history . . .

APPENDIXES

APPENDIXES

A/

Comparative
Naval Strengths

TYPE	ARGENTINA		BRITAIN[1,2,3] (IN AREA)	
Conventional Aircraft Carrier	1	carrying 12 A-4s 4 helos 6 S-2s	0	
VSTOL Aircraft Carrier	0		2	carrying Harriers carrying helos
Auxiliary VSTOL Carrier	0		2	(–1, sunk) carrying Harriers carrying helos
Cruiser	1 (sunk)		0	
Destroyer	9		5 (–2)	
Frigate/Corvette	5		14 (–2)	
Attack Submarine				
Nuclear-powered	0		2-5 (?)	
Diesel-powered	4 (–1)		1	
Amphibious Warfare Ship	2		2	

Major Combatants Only, original count.

? Number uncertain.

Notes: 1. These figures total between one-half and two-thirds of Britain's combatant surface navy.
2. "In area" indicates ships at Ascension or farther south.
3. Replacements and additions arrived in a steady stream.

Comparative Air Strengths

TYPE	ARGENTINA[1, 2, 3]	BRITAIN[5]
Heavy Bomber	9 Canberra	? Vulcan (operating from Britain via Ascension one at a time)
Fighter/Interceptor	44 ? Mirage III and Dagger	0
Attack (light bomber)	82 ? A-4 6 Super Etendard	24 – 36 (?) Harrier
Maritime Patrol	4 P-2H 6 S-2	5 Nimrod (fitted for aerial refueling; operating from Ascension)
Helicopter	58 ? (including 20 gunships)	42 (?) (including Lynx, Wasp, Sea King, Wessex, Gazelle, Chinook)
Counterinsurgency	45 Pucara	0
Other (Trainers, Transports, etc.)	?	? Hercules ? Victor
	230 ?[4]	83 ?

Notes: 1. No distinction is made here between aircraft of the Argentine air force and those of their naval air arm.
2. An Argentine 75 percent operational readiness rate would be good; the rate decreased as time went on.
3. Perhaps one-third of the approximately 140 Argentine high performance jets were lost.
4. The Argentines pressed many civilian aircraft into service, inflating many aircraft numbers.
5. British figures only account for aircraft in area, on Ascension or farther south.

C/

Chronology
(1982)

DATE	EVENT
18 March	Argentine salvors on South Georgia to dismantle old whaling station and hoist the Argentine flag.
1 April	Britain calls emergency meeting of the U.N. Security Council. Argentina begins clandestine landings in Falkland Islands.
2 April	Argentina seizes Falklands.
3 April	Argentina seizes South Georgia. Britain announces a task force.
4 April	Britain begins to assemble a naval task force and to charter/requisition merchant vessels.
5 April	Lead echelon of Falklands task force sails.
8 April	Britain announces a total blockade of the islands. Argentina does the same against British ships.
9 April	3 Commando Brigade/*Canberra* sail.
12 April	200-mile maritime exclusion zone comes into effect. Submarine *Spartan* arrives off Stanley.
16 April	Task force sails from Ascension Island.
21 April	Task force sighted by Argentine reconnaissance.
23 April	Argentina warned that any threat to the force would be dealt with.
25 April	Marines recapture South Georgia; Argentine submarine *Santa Fe* attacked and forced aground, sunk.
30 April	Total exclusion zone comes into effect.
late April -early May	Picket line between mainland and islands formed.
1 May	First air attacks on Argentine positions in islands. Argentine air attacks begin.
2 May	Argentine cruiser *General Belgrano* torpedoed by British submarine, subsequently sank.
4 May	British destroyer, *Sheffield* hit by missle, subsequently sank.

C/CHRONOLOGY (1982) (Continued)

7 May	Britain announces naval and air blockade of Argentine mainland; any warship or aircraft over 12 miles from the Argentine coast would be regarded as hostile.
9 May	Frigate penetrates Falkland Sound without opposition.
11 May	*Isla de los Estados* sunk by gunfire from British frigate.
14 May	British raid Argentine installations on Pebble Island.
21 May	First main landing of British troops (3 Commando Brigade) at San Carlos on East Falkland. "Gunline" set up. British frigate *Ardent* sunk.
23 May	British frigate *Antelope* hit, sunk the following day.
25 May	British destroyer *Coventry* bombed, subsequently sunk; British auxiliary aircraft carrier *Atlantic Conveyor* hit by missile, sunk.
1 June	5 Infantry Brigade lands at San Carlos.
8 June	RFAs *Sir Galahad* and *Sir Tristram* attacked with bombs and rockets and set afire; *Galahad* sunk; *Tristram* constructive total loss.
11 June	*Glamorgan* damaged by shore-based Exocet—the last naval casualty of the war.
14 June	Argentine forces in islands surrender; 11,400 prisoners taken. Falklands return to British rule.
20 June	South Thule secured.
14 July	Last Argentine prisoners returned home.

D/

Argentina's Fighting Fleet

TASK FORCE MEMBERS AFTER APRIL 5

TF 79	Task Force 79 (RADM Gualter Allara)
TG 79.1	*25 de Mayo* *Trinidad* 3 corvettes (*Drummond, Granville,* *Guerrico*) oiler
TG 79.2	(*Bouchard*) (*Piedrabuena*) *Py* *Segui* *Hercules* oiler
TG 79.3	*General Belgrano* *Bouchard* *Piedrabuena* oiler

Note: *Bouchard* and *Piedrabuena* were apparently escorts for *Belgrano* until *Belgrano* sank; they then rejoined TG 79.2.

On May 1, the fleet commander ordered the three corvettes and an oiler constituted TG 79.4, a possible additional antisurface group.

169

The Royal Navy Contribution

TYPE	NAME	COMMENT
Small Aircraft Carriers (CVL/CVE)	*Hermes*	fleet flagship
	Invincible	
Destroyers (DD)	*Antrim*	damaged
	Glamorgan	damaged
	Bristol	
	Cardiff	
	Coventry	sunk, hit by bombs
	Exeter	
	Glasgow	badly damaged
	Sheffield	sunk, hit by Exocet
Frigates (FF)	*Active*	
	Alacrity	
	Ambuscade	
	Antelope	sunk, hit by dud bomb which exploded while being defuzed
	Ardent	sunk, hit by bombs and rockets
	Arrow	damaged
	Avenger	
	Brilliant	damaged
	Broadsword	damaged
	Andromeda	
	Argonaut	badly damaged
	Minerva	
	Penelope	
	Plymouth	damaged
	Yarmouth	

E/THE ROYAL NAVY CONTRIBUTION (Continued)

Submarines (SSK)	*Spartan*	the first five are
	Splendid	nuclear powered
	Courageous	
	Conqueror	
	Valiant	
	Onyx	diesel powered
Amphibious Warfare Ships (LPD)	*Fearless*	broad pennant of commodore amphibious warfare
	Intrepid	
Offshore Patrol Vessels (OPV)	*Leeds Castle*	dispatch vessels
	Dumbarton Castle	
Mine Countermeasure Ships (MCM)	*Northella*	all five are
	Farnella	STUFT, com-
	Junella	missioned and
	Cordella	given RN crews
	Pict	(former deepsea trawlers)
Antarctic Support Ship (AGB)	*Endurance*	
Survey Ships (AGS)	*Hecla*	hospital ships/
	Herald	casualty ferries
	Hydra	

Task Force Members, count to mid-June

F/

The Royal Fleet Auxiliary Contribution

TYPE	NAME	COMMENT
Landing Ships, Logistic* (LSL)	*Sir Bedivere*	
	Sir Galahad	sunk, hit by bombs and rockets
	Sir Geraint	
	Sir Lancelot	damaged
	Sir Percivale	
	Sir Tristram	damaged (beached, a constructive total loss)
Oilers (AO)	*Olmeda*	
	Olna	
	Tidepool	strengthened for ice operations
	Tidespring	
	Appleleaf	
	Bayleaf	
	Brambleleaf	
	Pearleaf	
	Plumleaf	
	Blue Rover	
Replenishment Ships (AEFS)	*Fort Austin*	broad pennant of commodore RFA
	Fort Grange	
	Resource	
	Regent	
	Stromness	
Helicopter Support Ship (ARVH)	*Engadine*	

Task Force Members, Final Count
*These ships retained their original Chinese crews and British officers.

172

The Merchant Navy Contribution[1, 2, 3,]

SHIP'S NAME	TYPE
Queen Elizabeth 2	passenger liner/trooper
Canberra	passenger liner/trooper
Atlantic Conveyor	auxiliary carrier; sunk, hit by Exocet; combination ro-ro/container ship
Atlantic Causeway	auxiliary carrier; combination ro-ro/container ship
Uganda	school cruise/hospital ship
Norland	passenger/vehicle ro-ro ferry
Rangitira	passenger/cargo ship
St. Edmund	passenger/vehicle ro-ro ferry
Tor Calendonia	ro-ro ferry
Elk	ro-ro ferry
Contender Bezant	ro-ro ferry
Astronomer	container ship
Nordic Ferry	ro-ro ferry
Baltic Ferry	ro-ro ferry
Europic Ferry	ro-ro ferry
British Avon	tanker
British Dart	tanker
British Esk	tanker
British Tamar	tanker
British Tay	tanker
British Test	tanker
British Trent	tanker
British Wye	tanker
Balder London	tanker
G. A. Walker	tanker

Scottish Eagle	tanker
Alvega	tanker
Anco Charger	chemical tanker
Shell Eburna	tanker
Lycaon	freighter
Laertes	freighter
Geestport	reefer; general cargo
Fort Toronto	water tanker
St. Helena	passenger/cargo ship; trawler mother ship
Saxonia	freighter; reefer
Stena Seaspread	salvage and maintenance ship
Stena Inspector	salvage and maintenance ship
Strathewe	freighter
Avelona Star	freighter
Iris	cableship
Yorkshireman	tug
Irishman	tug
Salvageman	tug
Wimpey Seahorse	tug
British Enterprise III	diving support ship

Notes: **1.** No "third party" interest ships are likely to have gone south of Ascension.

2. The government appears to have continued to requisition a number of ships even after hostilities ended.

3. Several ships were found unsuited, and released at once.

H/

British Naval
Missiles (Tactical)

MISSILE	PLATFORM	CHARACTERISTICS
Sea Dart	new destroyers and *Invincibles*	surface-to-surface and anti-air long range (20-miles) area defense; radar-homing
Seawolf	new frigates (*Broadswords* and some late *Leanders*)	anti-air short range (4-miles) point defense; fully computerized, responding automatically when radar identifies a threat; radar-homing
Sidewinder	Harriers	air-to-air; heat seeking
Sea Skua	Lynx helos	air-to-surface; designed for use against small surface ships and craft such as fast patrol boats; sea-skimming; radar-homing; range 9 miles
Sea Cat	older destroyers and frigates	anti-air short range (3-miles) point defense; radar or optical guidance; being phased out
Ikara	destroyers and frigates	long range ASW weapon system; missile-launched torpedo effective to 9 miles
Exocet	destroyers and frigates	surface-to-surface MM 38; inertial mid-course guidance, terminal radar-homing; long range (30-miles)

Notes: Arranged by frequency of use in the Falkland War.

I/
The Falklands Situation

THE FALKLANDS — SITUATION
Late May - Early June

J/
Falklands Victory Message

Headquarters Land Forces Falkland Islands, Port Stanley. In Port Stanley at 9 o'clock p.m. Falkland Islands time tonight 14 June 1982, Major-General Menendez surrendered to me all the Argentine Armed Forces in East and West Falkland, together with their impediments.

Arrangements are in hand to assemble the men for return to Argentina, to gather in their arms and equipment, and to make safe their munitions.

The Falkland Islands are once more under the government desired by their inhabitants.

God save the Queen.   J. J. Moore

Selected Bibliography

BOOKS

Bishop, Patrick, and Witherow, John. *The Winter War*. London: Quartet Books, 1982.

Corbett, Julian S. *Some Principles of Maritime Strategy*. Annapolis: Naval Institute Press, 1972.

Couhat, Jean Labayle (ed.) *Combat Fleets of the World 1982-83*. Annapolis: Naval Institute Press, 1982.

Fox, Robert. *Eyewitness Falklands*. London: Methuen, 1982.

Fox, Robert, and Hanrahan, Brian. *"I Counted Them All Out and I Counted Them All Back."* London: British Broadcasting Corporation, 1982.

Hastings, Max, and Jenkins, Simon. *The Battle for the Falklands*. London: Michael Joseph, 1983. Also New York: W. W. Norton, 1983.

Laffin, John. *Fight for the Falklands*! New York: St. Martin's Press, 1982.

Luttwak, Edward N. *The Political Uses of Sea Power*. Baltimore: Johns Hopkins University Press, 1974.

Macintyre, Donald. *Narvik*. London: Pan Books, 1962.

Ministry of Defence. *The Falklands Campaign: The Lessons*. London: Her Majesty's Stationary Office, 1982.

Morison, Samuel Eliot. *The Two-Ocean War*. Boston: Little, Brown, 1963.

Perrett, Bryan. *Weapons of the Falklands Conflict*. Poole: Blandford Press, 1982.

Preston, Antony. *Sea Combat Off the Falklands*. London: Willow Books, 1982.

Speed, Keith. *Sea Change*. Bath: Ashgrove Press, 1982.

Sunday Times. *War in the Falklands*. New York: Harper and Row, 1982.

Taffrail [pseud.]. *Endless Story*. London: Hodder and Stoughton, 1938.

NEWSPAPERS AND PERIODICALS

Fieldhouse, John. "Despatch," *The London Gazette* (13 December 1982).

"The Malvinas Conflict: 1982," *Gaceta Marinera* (December 1982). Published in Buenos Aires. Special English language edition.

Nott, John. "The Falklands Campaign," U.S. Naval Institute *Proceedings* (May 1983) 118-139.

Scheina, Robert L. "The Malvinas Campaign," U.S. Naval Institute *Proceedings* (May 1983) 98-117.

OTHER PUBLISHED MATERIAL

British Aerospace. *V/STOL In the Roaring Forties.* Kingston Upon Thames: British Aerospace, 1983.

English, Adrian, and Watts, Anthony. *Battle For The Falklands (2) Naval Forces.* London: Osprey, 1982.

Index

182

184

About the Author

CAPTAIN C.W. KOBURGER, JR., U.S. Coast Guard Reserve, retired, is by profession an independent consultant (research analyst) in the operational aspects of maritime affairs. With a background in port security, aids to navigation, and marine inspection, he took 33 years to collect 20 years active duty. He was Omega's management and budget officer for two years, assembling Omega's first full budget. Since retirement, he has completed accident investigations for Liberia; consulted on navigation equipment design and bridge layout, and VTS (vessel traffic system(s)). He has been named a visiting professor at the United Nations' World Maritime University (Malmo) and research fellow at London Polytechnic. Captain Koburger is a regular graduate of the Armed Forces Staff College. A Companion of the (British) Nautical Institute, he has contributed over 50 articles to professional journals on both sides of the Atlantic. He was national marine chairman of the Institute of Navigation (ION) 1979–81.

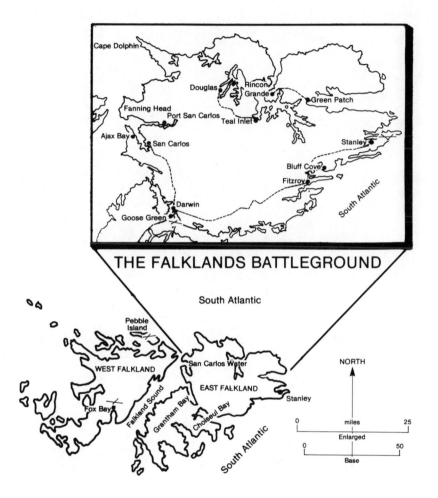

THE FALKLANDS BATTLEGROUND

Cape Dolphin

Douglas   Rincon
Grande
Fanning Head   Green Patch
Port San Carlos
Teal Inlet
Ajax Bay
San Carlos   Stanley
Bluff Cove
Fitzroy
Darwin   South Atlantic
Goose Green

South Atlantic

Pebble
Island
San Carlos Water
WEST FALKLAND
EAST FALKLAND
Fox Bay   Stanley
Falkland Sound
Grantham Bay
Choiseul Bay
South Atlantic

NORTH

0	miles	25
Enlarged

0		50
Base